THE LAST ALCHEMIST

THE LAST ALCHEMIST

*Ancient Hermetic
Wisdom
for a Modern Life*

C JON SAWYER

CHAPTER 1

Dedication

I first 'met' Sol in my dreams. He came to me several times and took me to his world so that I might swim in the pools at the bottom of the waterfall, lay on the secluded grassy rest areas, and chat with him and the other 'guides' about the nature of life. I also called on him several times when I was frightened or in need. In all cases, he came and stood with me. The first time I took an Ayahuasca journey, I had all control stripped from me and was so overwhelmed at not having a sense of direction. During those moments, I physically saw Sol and Mara standing in the room with me watching over me.

This book is dedicated to Sol, Mara, and all the other guides of the human race that work tirelessly to ensure we stay connected and on the Path.

Firstly, I would like to dedicate this book to my beautiful and very talented Daughter, Trinity Rose. Trinity, if I could give you any gift in this world, it would be the knowing that anything is possible. Follow your heart, Darling!

I would like to also dedicate to my mother, without whom this story would not be possible. For being instrumental in my development, I give a massive thanks.

I dedicate this book to my father, for his constant presence in my life. He has always been there for me, and I feel that even after he has departed this world he will continue to be, standing beside Sol and Mara as a guide to this race.

Lastly and most importantly, I want to dedicate this book to my amazing Wife, Lindsay. She has stood in the fire beside me constantly, and I am everything that I am in life because of her. She is the Divine Feminine to my Sacred Masculine and for the perfection in this, I give a huge thanks. I love you Boo!

CHAPTER 2

Prologue

"If you're going through hell... keep going."
Winston Churchill

I would love to say that my path in this lifetime has been a charmed one. It would be amazing to sit here and somehow manage to write to you that due to the work I had already done in previous incarnations, I had a perfect story this time around and that it unfolded in a calm and peaceful manner. Realistically, not a single one of us can say such a thing.

Even those of us born with the Master Path of the Alchemist already complete inside of us have to remember that we did in fact walk the path. We are NOT born here as gold, without the need for the work once again.

The story that you are about to read is a blend. It contains elements of the path that this particular Alchemist walked in order to remember his gold-like nature, mingled with channeled wisdom that needed to be written. Most of the journey toward creating this story was undertaken in an altered state of consciousness; what the main character experienced, I was fortunate enough to have experienced. I remember being pulled along and drawn in from the time I sat down and started typing until hours later when the need to attend to some other aspect of mundane life returned.

The way this story asked me to write it allows you, the reader, to be drawn in and experience the adventure first-hand in just the same way. My friends, you have come a very long way to arrive at this point, and now it is time to start making sense of that journey.

This book is written for you so that you may do just that very thing. This is your story. A story of adventure and intrigue and as you read, I know that you will find yourself in a world more real than the reality we currently call home; just as I did when I wrote it. So dive in, let go, and allow yourself to transmute into the gold that you already are.

C. Jon Sawyer

CHAPTER 3

We all begin as lead

"Begin, be bold, and venture to be wise."
Horace

It started exactly the same way as it always does. The intrusive, annoying sound of his alarm dragging him from a halfway peaceful slumber back into the cold reality of his life. Although he rarely slept well, it was still a time of respite, a space where the crowds and the advertising and the dross of the modern-day world could not touch. It was his final frontier. Of course, he had tried the various "peaceful" sounds that were meant to gently coax one awake, yet he quickly came to understand that it wasn't so much the sound itself that made it annoying and intrusive to him... It was merely the fact that he was being forced back into the waking world—a world full of light, sound, mayhem, and life!

His slowly dawning consciousness brought with it the all too familiar feeling of a deep rut; a feeling that walking through the exact same routine every single day had slowly worn into the folds and creases of his life. The routine he had grown to despise from the very core of his being. *Pour the coffee, water the plants, shower, get dressed, make lunch, and then the worst of all... the hour-long struggle down the overcrowded 405 motorway to a job that only mildly amused him at best. Work all day, come home, make dinner, watch Netflix, and fall asleep on the couch. Stumble half asleep into his bed and drift off realizing that tomorrow was an exact carbon copy of what had just happened.*

Where was the magic? When did he become little more than a cog, ground down slowly by the inescapable machine that he was now a part of?

There was no definitive line where he stopped enjoying his journey, no point where he stepped from an amazing life into the doldrums. It wasn't as if one minute he was enjoying himself, and the next he wasn't. It was much more of a gradual, almost imperceptible slide downwards.

He remembered reading a quote somewhere: "The chains of habit are often too soft to be felt until they are too strong to be broken." A paradigm identical in nature to the proverbial frog, which when placed into a pot of boiling water will jump right back out. However, if the frog is placed into a pot of cold water that's brought slowly to a boil, it will enjoy the jacuzzi until the moment it literally boils to death.

For him, it was the ever-delicate transition from creative writing, exercising, eating well, and intelligent conversation with close friends to couch surfing, TV series, fast food, and isolation that created the downward slide. Whereas once he had taken his time in deliberate action with almost every aspect of his life, stopping to smell the flowers and delight in the small but definite beauty that existed all around, he now floated along on autopilot, rarely knowing on a conscious level how he got from point A to point B.

Somewhere along the tedious commute on this particular morning, he had a brief but powerful recollection of a dream that he had experienced throughout the night. Normally, the process of his mind fluttering from this thought to that while he floated through the routine of his existence was fairly commonplace these days. However, this one thought stood out because he noted with some curiosity that the dream in question had reoccurred several times over the past few weeks.

It always started the same... He was in the wilderness in what seemed to be the Pacific Northwest, surrounded by various giant fir trees. The details of the dream were always so vivid, the dreamscape itself so alive to him that even after waking he could still taste, in the depths of his sinuses, the rich tree resin, feel the cool air upon his skin, hear the crunching of fallen pine needles under his footfall.

Each time he had dreamt of being in this place, the feeling was the same: there was a deep feeling of home, a sense of belonging that he had never really known in his life. There was a calling within him towards a snow-capped mountain that stood in the middle of it all, and as he left his camp and approached the mountain, he felt guided toward a particular trail that wound around the base, slowly and steadily making its way upward.

He would always arrive at a junction point somewhere along the path that was crowded with people. He was curiously aware that the people were not quite real though, appearing to him as shadows or manifestations of various energy. Some spoke in hushed and reverent tones of the sacred magic the place contained, while others were warning him to turn back, that the path ahead was blocked and he could not successfully make the pass. There were whispers of an ensuing darkness which stated that it would be a dangerous place once it had arrived. In all cases, he only ever stood listening to them for the briefest of moments before continuing onward and upward.

As he progressed, he passed by monks in brightly colored robes, meditating along cliff tops, seated in and around various monasteries. He saw etched into the rocks along the path different power symbols; some he recognized, some were vague and obscure to him.

Finally, he came upon a place that was unlike anything he had ever seen. There was a series of waterfalls, cutting through the rocks and dropping into crystal clear pools. Although that in and of itself was not particularly unique, the thing about this place was that all the water from the falls and in the pools appeared to be hot springs. There was steam rising up off the surface of the water, mingling into the cold mountain air.

Whether it was because of the hot springs, or by the hand of something else, the entire area surrounding the falls and pools was lush and tropical in stark contrast to the snow, ice, and rock of the mountain. It was as if two different artists had contributed to the painting of the landscape, one portraying a warm tropical paradise, one expressing an icy mountain pass. The thing that he noted was, for whatever reason, it WORKED! The place felt as natural to him as the park several blocks from his house would on a Sunday afternoon stroll. He purposefully removed all of his clothes and slowly eased himself into the warmth of the first pool. He noted that the water didn't just engulf his naked body, surrounding his skin in warm softness just the way a hot spring would, but that it actually delighted in doing so. The water was alive and he could almost hear it singing with pleasure at being able to interact with and serve him.

And then, just like that it was gone. That pleasant, annoying alarm tone that dragged him from the Grace of such a profound space back into a world that didn't make any sense.

His musings about this powerful, repetitive dream were cut short as the traffic ahead of him came to a grinding halt like it frequently did on the i-405 for absolutely no reason at all. And with that, he was no longer an intrepid explorer on the path to Shambhala; he was once again nothing more than a cog in a giant machine that grinds people down into husks of themselves. Rolling onto the next random thought, he realized that it was Tuesday and that meant only one thing to him; tonight after work was his weekly session with his counselor.

CHAPTER 4

The map

"If you do not change direction, you may end up where you are heading."`
Lao Tzu

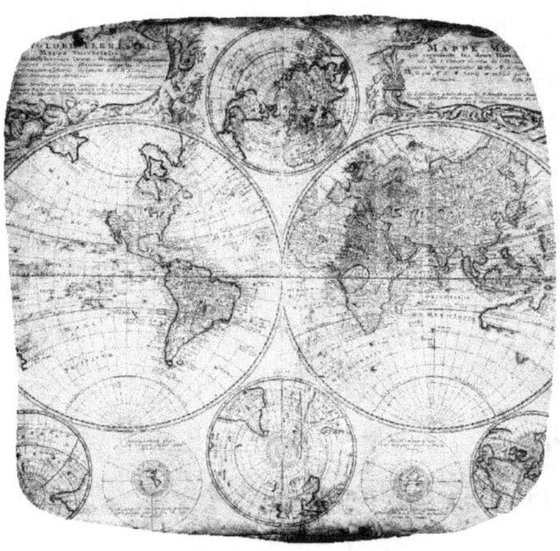

As he drove from work to the counselor's office, he tried to calm himself with some relaxing music and breathing techniques that he'd read about. However, pitching the music and his breathing against the madness of greater L.A. traffic was akin to an infant trying to fight Muhammad Ali. As much as he wanted to appear to the counselor as calm and relaxed, it was a losing battle, and he knew it.

"What did it matter anyway?" he mumbled to himself as he pulled into her parking lot.

After a brief wait, he found himself seated across from the youngish, plump girl who was staring uncomfortably at him. "Did you hear my question?"

"Sorry, no. I was somewhere else just now. Ask me again."

"I wanted to explore your ability to forge quality relationships a little more and asked you about the time your parents had separated."

"I don't really know what to tell you. I remember fragments of it. During my seventh birthday, I was sitting at the dinner table with my father and brother, yet my mother was nowhere to be found. I remember Dad handing me a postage pack, which had some gifts in it from her. She'd clearly taken a little time to send me something from wherever she had decided to go and allow her reality to unfold."

"It sounds like you may have a little resentment over her not being present at that time."

"Maybe. I guess it's possible. Although honestly, I can't remember feeling too perturbed by her absence at the time. I mean, I was a child and didn't understand the complexities or dynamics of adult relationships. I *did* have a postage pack with gifts, and *was* eating my favorite meal. All in all, it was *my* night and I was a little too lost in that. I was the special one because it was *my* birthday."

"Yes, but looking back, how do you think it impacted you?"

He sat in contemplation for a moment, and what he said next almost felt as though something else was speaking through him, using his voice to purvey a level of wisdom that he didn't know he possessed.

"It was very possibly the moment I was struck with the realization that we live in a world of potentiality."

There was an awkward pause as if he had said something that he didn't fully understand and frantically tried to find a way to explain.

"I guess that up until that point everything was possible for me. I had never had thoughts before that there might have to be correct conditions or parameters for something to occur; that if something had the potential to exist, it also had the potential not to.

Until that point, I wasn't able to think in terms of what was potential, what was possible, and what was probable. Everything was merely possible! There was nothing else. I mean, I knew in my heart that I wanted my mother to be there with us, happily sharing dinner as a family. Maybe even deeper I also knew I just wanted her to be happy and if that happiness wasn't to be found within the confines of a relationship she shared with my father, then it truly was more important for her peace of mind to be elsewhere."

As he spoke, he started to realize that the events of this one, simple evening while sitting at a dinner table one parent shy - a situation well outside the scope of control or understanding of a child - had created the beginning of a process for him. It was the start of a chain of events that would lead him down a path of no return.

"I think you've had a breakthrough tonight. Well done. We're out of time now, but I look forward to exploring this more next week."

The end of the session always felt a little cold to him. Right as he was getting into a flow, taking the journey inward and making progress, she shut it down, asked for payment, and then bid him farewell.

"Oh well, there's always next week," he mumbled to himself as he pulled out of her parking lot.

The remainder of the week held absolutely no intrigue or break from the routine save for one thing; he had his recurring dream another two times. Each time he awoke from his visit to what he was calling "Shambhala," he found himself more disappointed to be back in his own life than the previous time. As much as he loved his brief moments there on that unusual mountain, the jolt back to the reality of his life was almost painful. The allure of this magical dream world was becoming stronger, and it was very quickly becoming all he could think about throughout his day.

CHAPTER 5

The Mountains

"The mountains are calling, and I must go."
John Muir

One evening after work he decided to do a little offhand research on the mountains of the Pacific Northwest. Googling the Cascade Range, he took a virtual tour over Mt. Rainier, Mt. Hood, Mt. Saint Helens, and Mt. Adams. Although they were all a very pretty part of this world, and he made mental notes to try and spend a little time visiting these places, none of them particularly stood out to him. When he reached the Southern part of the Range and stumbled onto a photo of Mt. Shasta, his heart skipped a beat and he almost choked on the very air he was currently inhaling. *Shasta! It can't be!* Yet he knew in his heart of hearts that he was looking at the very same mountain from his dreamscape.

With the frequency of his dream, it didn't take all that much self-convincing to leave work early on Friday, unload the dusty storage box that contained his camping gear, and take a weekend road-trip. After all, he used to do this sort of thing all the time. He knew more about the wonders of such wild places as Joshua Tree, Death Valley, and Big Sur than he did about the city he had called home for the past two and a half years. He had become quite the recluse in order to avoid the noise, the crowds, and the dirty nature of L.A., and he found that his trips away to the beautiful wilderness also ceased.

It was so much easier to struggle for a parking space only once on a Friday evening after work, and then lock himself in and do absolutely nothing all weekend than it was to endure the efforts to be out and exploring. So, this became his routine. The routine that he couldn't feel the weight of until the strength of it was almost too much to break free from.

He arrived home just after lunch on Friday afternoon and went straight to the cupboard under the stairs that housed his camping and climbing gear. Checking out everything with as much care as he could muster, he packed his little one-person tent, hiking stove, and Therm-A-Rest bed roll into his backpack. He grabbed a few items of food from the pantry that he thought would be sufficient for two days, and then carried the lot out to his car which was parked illegally on a red curb with its hazard lights flashing - the international symbol for "I'm loading my car" in Long Beach.

He spent almost two hours trying to get clear of the city. As the road opened up ahead of him and became progressively free from the clutter of commuting motorists, his own thoughts started to do the exact same thing. His mind started slowing down and becoming less frantic.

He found himself immensely grateful for this strange recurring dream and the power it seemed to hold over his thoughts. Without it, he may never have broken free of the routine that he was progressively becoming a slave to. Even if nothing else came from it, the dream coaxed him from his rut and back into a life that involved weekend adventure. For the first time in months, he felt as though he could take a deep breath and he relaxed back into the car seat as he exhaled.

The time passed easily and the drive north was relatively uneventful. He wasn't expecting any real excitement; other than the radio and a few cups of bad truck stop coffee, the miles dissolved without much ado. He played over in his mind the last conversation he had with his counselor, and recalled the way he had strangely spoken those words about potentiality. *What did it all mean anyway? Did it have something to do with the dreams?* Many questions fluttered across the landscape of his mind as he drove headlong toward the township of Shasta.

Although he had set off from L.A. at 8 p.m. and was expecting approximately 10 hours of driving time, he got caught in heavy traffic on the I5 motorway leaving LA, which put him several hours behind. On top of this, a little later in the evening he got a tire puncture somewhere along the way on a random stretch of desolate highway.

He had never had a tire puncture in his life. For some strange reason right at that moment in the middle of the night, as he went through the routine of setting up the jack, loosening the wheel nuts, and changing the tire, the words of one shadowy, faceless person from the mountain path in his dream flashed across his mind. The figure was standing at the junction of the trail, pointing upward and saying to him, "The path ahead is blocked and you will not successfully make the pass."

He shuddered as he pushed the thought from his mind. He carefully finished tightening the wheel nuts, lowered the jack and slowly made his way to his feet. Taking a brief moment before getting back into his car, he looked out into the paddocks of farmland surrounding him and he was immediately overwhelmed by the vast openness and blanket of stars overhead.

Throughout much of the drive his mind drifted from thought to thought. He remembered various events from his childhood, different girlfriends he had been enamored with. He thought about the few pets he had loved, and the many jobs he had hated.

He neither clung to nor chased these thoughts and memories; he just allowed them to flow. This was a relatively unusual experience for him. He often found that when he had quiet time away from distraction, he would become a control freak; pursuing certain thoughts, forcing his mind in a particular direction for one reason or another, and then struggle to hold onto and direct these thoughts as they would naturally try to dissipate.

During the early hours of the morning, he remembered a time when his life had changed abruptly and permanently. He was 11 years old when he discovered that his mother was having an extramarital affair. He had always been really good at finding out the how and why for everything. This skill-set had even brought him some small pocket change as he sold his abilities to the other kids in the neighborhood for gossip, or finding things that had become lost.

He was an grade-A snoop, and unfortunately this very attribute was one that he had grown quite proud of, but it ended up creating a turn in his life. One he still wished to this day had not occurred.

He didn't know when his mother had started seeing other men. Perhaps it was one of the three times that his parents had separated since the night at the dinner table on his seventh birthday. As good as he was at discovering things, he was even better at keeping secrets when there was no good to come from divulging them.

In this instance, he kept his mother's secret for two long years, sitting in the knowledge that when his father left for work, she would make herself available to other men. Business trips for her were code for hotel rooms and pleasure. Although the term "infidelity" had never fallen upon his young ears at this point of his life, he knew in his heart of hearts that what was happening wasn't right.

Although they were not really all that connected, he loved his father. He always saw him as a simple yet strong, easygoing and unassuming man who worked hard and kept his head down. He found himself smiling at the realization that he had never once seen his father drunk or abusive. Yes, he was a good man indeed.

As it was, seeing the man who worked hard to provide for his family, who worked hard at being a dedicated father and respectable husband, betrayed in such a way was a slow heartbreak for him over two years. He couldn't have known it at the time, but in keeping his mother safe by holding her little secret, the softness of his own heart was slowly turning hard.

He wasn't entirely sure his father was unaware of what was going on, but after having this horrible seed inside of him grow bigger for two long years he simply couldn't take it anymore. His father needed to know what was happening within his household, and by God, for better or for worse, in the absence of anyone else stepping forward to do it, he was going to be the one that told him.

He remembered with vivid clarity the event of the day he decided to make the affair known. Everything that sat outside of the event itself, however, remained hidden in a hazy darkness of obscurity. As he reached his hand from the steering wheel to touch the window glass - a mindless gesture to feel the temperature outside the car - he mused briefly that this might often be the case with traumatic events. The memory continued to play out for him as his eleven-year-old self asked his mother and father to come into the lounge room so that he could tell them something.

What were they expecting? There was a certain nervous anticipation on their faces, the kind that any parent gets when their child is ready to talk about drug use, gang violence, or pregnancy. Needless to say, when it came out of his young mouth that his mother had been having an affair for the past two years, for several moments the air hung heavy like a cloud of damp, bone chilling mist over a seaside village in winter.

He remembered the reality of it slowly dawning on his father. The way the older man looked in the direction of his wife, almost begging her to deny it. The way that when the denial of it never came, he dropped his head into his hands and started sobbing. He remembered in exact detail how it was his words, his young voice that thrust the knife of someone else's making into his father's heart. Although he did not forge the weapon, he had been the one to wield it. He didn't know if it was the thought itself, the long lonely drive on an isolated stretch of highway, or the early hour of the morning, but he shuddered involuntarily.

Next came his mother's reaction... As much as he was screaming inside of himself that he wanted her to look him in the eyes, hug him, and tell him he had done the right thing; that as hard as it had been, he had been mature and brave in stepping forward with the truth, it did not go down like that. No, he remembered his mother looking him right in the eyes and saying to him with a strong dose of overwhelming pain in her voice that he had just ruined her life, right before standing up and storming out of the room. It was at this point that the memory always faded, the scene darkening just like in a stage production.

The drive toward Shasta grew from ordinary to spectacular. As dawn arrived, grazing land gave way to old forests, and sea level gave way to altitude. The white peak of the mountain rose up above all else in the distance and hung in the sky ahead of him for a good hour as he drove the final miles. He finally arrived into the quiet little township just before noon, and took the opportunity to grab a quick lunch from a quaint little cafe. He always delighted in kitchen cooked food before and after any time in the wild, usually selecting anything he was unable to make on his little camp stove. Washing down his meal of vegetarian lasagna and a side of cornbread with a nice, hot coffee, he set out to find the ranger station.

In such a small town it didn't take long before he was chatting with a young woman dressed in ranger attire. They spoke about the various spots where he could camp, and about the legalities of actually climbing the upper peaks of Mt. Shasta. He gratefully accepted a map from her and left the station, driving up the road that led toward the various camping areas. At the suggestion of the young ranger, he parked his car at Bunny Flats, which was the highest point he could reach with the vehicle. Then, locking up his car and donning his pack, he walked the rest of the way to his destination, Panther Meadows, which sat at 7,400 feet.

Although it had been months since he had used any of his camping equipment, it was the one thing he had always been meticulous about looking after. He would never have his car serviced in time. He would always wait until a house plant started dying before he thought to care for it. Yet, his old outdoor gear was still in near new condition. To him, it had always been his key to escaping the grind, his escape from a reality of concrete and smog so it made sense to take care of it. Somewhere in his mind there was a whisper of realization and he chuckled as it told him this was because he valued it, and when we value something, we tend to take care of it. He chuckled even further as he realized how many things in his life held little to no value to him as evidenced by his lack of ability to care for them.

He had also always taken a very soft approach when entering into the wilderness. Tread lightly, be a polite and courteous guest, find the balance that exists between all things, and stay within its boundaries. As such, he had never had any mishaps while outdoors and believed firmly that the respect he offered the wild world was returned to him. Again, came the realization spotlighting the difference between how he interacted with anything that he held a reverence for and that which he did not.

There was a time, not so long ago, that he would have raced to his camp site with the giddy excitement of a child waking up at the first sign of dawn on Christmas morning. He would have hastily set up his tent, and then used the remaining daylight to explore. It was different this time. He was exhausted to the very core of his being, and although the drive throughout the night had rendered him physically tired, what he was experiencing now, without the distraction of Netflix and his comfortable couch, was a pounding sensation that ran deep into his soul. If he was honest with himself, he had been feeling it for a long while now, but the distractions of the modern-day world were vast, plentiful, and very effective.

Although it was only mid-afternoon, he just slumped on the ground staring at the pristine and majestic mountain in a kind of daze, the fallen pine needles soft under the weight of his body. As he watched the afternoon sunlight glistening across the stunning peaks of the mountain, he heard the compulsive voice of his old explorer self-resonate from within as it pulled at him to do more than he was currently doing. *Look at that amazing place right there... get up and go revel in it.* With that, he grunted, laid down onto the blanket of pine needles, rolled onto his side with his arm under his head as a pillow, and fell immediately into a deep, dreamless sleep.

The Journey Inward

"We have two commodities that are worth more than anything else...
Our time and our peace.
Our time should never be sold cheaply, and our peace should never be
sold at all."
WARRIOR.PHILOSOPHICAL

He awoke startled in the night time woods. *What time was it? How long had he been asleep?* He could have sworn that he had laid down beside his tent for a brief nap only moments ago. Yet, it was daylight when he fell asleep, and now he was sitting in the dark against a fallen log alongside a trail with his hiking pack on. Had he awoken earlier and decided after all to go for a hike on the remaining afternoon sunlight? Was it possible that he had completely forgotten that he was hiking, sat down for a rest and drifted off again? It wouldn't be the first time he travelled on autopilot only to arrive somewhere with no conscious recollection of the actual trip.

He stood up to try and gain his bearings but immediately felt off balance, stumbling and falling in a heap back to the ground where he had just awoken. After a few moments on the ground, he opened his eyes again and saw that there was a person looking down upon him. Although he couldn't quite focus enough in the dark to ascertain whether they were male or female, he could feel a very strong sense of compassion emanating toward him. '*This past week has been really unusual*, he thought to himself. *Can it really get any more so at this point?'*

From within the confines of his own mind he heard a voice echo: '*Yes, and yes.'*

"Um, come again?" he spoke out loud.

The voice appeared from inside his head again: '*You thought to yourself that this past week had been really strange and we agreed that yes, it has been strange for you, and then you thought the question "can it really get any more so?" and we answered that YES, in fact it can, and it is about to.'*

"How are... um, how are you doing that? Have I finally lost my mind? Am I dreaming? What is this right now? I'm dreaming, aren't I?"

As if to reinforce that he was not actually going insane, the amount of compassion that he felt radiating from the stranger toward him increased exponentially. '*Please feel safe in the knowing that you have not lost your mind just yet. As to whether you are dreaming, well, would it matter if you were?'* He briefly cocked his head to one side and realized with a silly grin that it would not in fact matter in the slightest.

Although he could still not make out the stranger's face with any great detail in the cold, dark night, he could almost feel a smile on the soft words that were magically appearing in his head. '*You should also know that you need not speak any of your words out loud if you do not wish to. We are able to connect with everything that you think.'*

"So..." he started to say out loud, but then thought he'd try this on for size. *'So, you're telling me that... um, I'm sorry, this is crazy. You can really read my thoughts? I must be dreaming.'*

'Yes. We can read your thoughts. No, you are not crazy. Let us, however, talk about this dream that you keep mentioning. What makes you think that you are dreaming? Because you are experiencing something that you have never experienced before? By that definition, did you think you might have been dreaming the first time you drove a car? How about the first time you made love? Or the first time you ate chocolate? Watched a sunrise? Swam in the ocean? Walked barefoot on grass? Do you see our point? Perhaps the whole thing is a dream, all of life... perhaps it is not. Who are we to say? But please, do not assume you are dreaming merely because you are experiencing something that you have not experienced before.'

'Umm, ok. I see your point. But, you keep referring to "we," Who are we? I only see you.'

'Ah, strong observation my friend. Yet, you only know the half of it. There is much that you cannot yet see, however it is still all around you. You have also very recently discovered that physically speaking is not a requirement between you and me. Imagine for a moment that it is the same for my entire race and myself.'

"Your entire race? What do you mean your entire race? Who exactly the hell are you? Where am I? Where's my tent?"

He started climbing to his feet and found himself speaking out loud again, with a touch of panic creeping into his voice, all without really knowing why. Perhaps it was just the shock of this insane conversation he was having with a very unusual stranger in the middle of the night on a wilderness trail that he could not remember walking to.

For the first time since the encounter, the being in front of him spoke with a physical voice, and much to his surprise, it was neither male nor female, but a gentle, melodic combination of both.

"My friend, it is best for you to remain calm right now. You have many questions, all of which will be answered soon. We have much work to do, and not a great deal of time in which to do it. Please just know for now that you have been chosen as a vessel for bringing ancient wisdom into a world in desperate need of it. In real time, and according to the rest of the world, you will spend a single night with us. However, as time has come to mean nothing to us, we have learned to distort it. For you, it will appear as though you have spent 12 months with us. Do not try to understand this right now as it is beyond your ability to grasp it with your intellect. All of the answers are coming."

From the minute the being started speaking to him, he began feeling progressively calm. There was an energetic quality carried on the words of the stranger that had the power to make him become still within, and in surrendering to it, he returned to thinking his words rather than speaking them. *'So, what do I have to do?'*

"Very good, my friend. You have just surrendered to the choice. You first made the choice to walk this path without any knowledge of what it meant to do so when you decided to leave your home and come here. After hearing what I have told you, your willingness to do what you must is your surrender to the process. Rise up now and stand with me. We have a long journey tonight that will take us into the mountain, to the home of my people."

He climbed sheepishly to his feet and realized with a start that the being in front of him towered over his own height of 5 feet 9 inches. He wasn't the greatest at guessing details such as this, but he would have said that his new friend was easily a graceful 9 feet tall.

They started together up the trail, and he suspected that he was somehow on the trail from his dream. The compassionate voice sounded in his mind again: *'You are right about that. This place does not exist to the outside world. No one would find this trail for it exists beyond the* veil *that sits over your world. We have been sending you the vision of this place for some time now. You remember a repetitive dream that started several weeks ago. In reality, you have been having this same dream for most of your life. You have only recently come to a point within yourself where you are ready for what we are about to show you.'*

He thought about this in silence for a few moments, and then silently asked: *'What about the monks and the symbols that I saw along the path in my dream?'*

'*These elements are reflective of the collective wisdom from your world that has penetrated through the veil. Many have attempted to walk the path, yet few have succeeded. Those that do succeed, leave a piece of themselves along the way for others to follow. That has been shown to you in a way that you would understand, such as the monks and symbols that you saw. Everyone would see something different depending on their level of understanding.*'

They walked on in silence for some time. He wasn't sure how long they were actually on this trail, but it felt to him like hours. The voice of his strange new friend entered his mind again: '*Try not to think in terms of time passing by like you are used to doing. As I mentioned earlier, we have become masters of bending and distorting time to suit our own needs, and we are well and truly beyond the limitations of your world now. Your version of time is a very human creation; one that does not exist here.*

The process of walking this trail in order to get to our destination is for you and you alone, because your mind is still firmly anchored to the confines of a physical, third dimensional reality. If we were to just appear in our home, you would not be able to comprehend what was happening to you and you would have a mental break. As it was, you still had a hard enough time fathoming what was happening. Therefore, we walk until you have deemed we have traveled sufficiently far enough for you to be at peace with being in a new place.'

"I see. So, we walk as long as I need us to? I mean, that all kind of makes sense, I guess. You never told me who you are."

'*I have been called by many names, my friend, and appeared in different forms to people across the various ages. I have been known as Mu, Hermes, Thoth, Melchizedek, and Saint Germaine amongst others. However, you may simply call me Sol. I have been your guide throughout this lifetime, and you need to know that due to the current state of the world, you are the last to be guided in such a way. The last that will ever receive this wisdom.*'

He felt a lump appear in his throat at the thought. What did Sol mean by "due to the current state of the world, you are the last…?" The last what? He knew that the world was not in great condition, but there would always be a world, right? Always be people carrying on in the mundane yet chaotic way that only people can? Sol was correct; he had so many questions, and every time they conversed, it did nothing to answer any of them, yet somehow managed to create more.

He heard a chuckle in his mind and simply the words: *'Soon my friend. Very soon.'*

They walked on for a little while longer, and eventually he noticed that the trail ahead of them was beginning to change. At first, he couldn't quite put his finger on it, but then it dawned on him that everything was slowly becoming illuminated. The light had a different appearance to that of daybreak; it wasn't coming from an external source above, yet rather from within everything around them. It was difficult for him to comprehend what he was seeing at first, but as the light became brighter, he noticed with a mild euphoria that the rocks surrounding the trail all seemed to be delighting so much in being noticed by the travelers that their very humming caused them to vibrate at such a high rate, they glowed.

'Welcome home, my friend', came the voice inside his head. *'This place is actually not responding any differently to what nature in your own world does. It's just that here interaction with it is consciously celebrated, and as such, it interacts with us in return on an entirely different level. In your world, people largely ignore such things, and so they have stopped interacting with you.'*

Whether it was just a very clear explanation by his guide or this place gave him a heightened understanding of things, he was unsure. What he did know for certain was that it made absolute sense to him that all things tend to become brighter when noticed. Children are happier and more active when they have the undivided attention of an adult; dogs positively beam when they are being doted upon; even plants have been shown to grow stronger and healthier when spoken or sung to.

The two travelers came up over a rise on the trail, and what lay before them rendered him absolutely breathless. He was looking at the scene from his dreams with a pristine tropical jungle encapsulated in a valley by the rock and ice of the mountain. Seated in the middle of it all were the hot spring waterfalls, and dotted throughout the jungle were patches of soft, well-manicured green grass that served as rest areas for the residents of this place.

Sol went on to explain: '*We don't sleep here. Because there is no time, there are no cycles of day and night as you know them. Everything glows from within creating a constant state of illumination. However, when you want to take rest, you go to one of the grassy areas and you'll find that as long as you need it to be so, things are exactly as you need them.*'

"I don't see all that many rest areas. What if all the grassy spots are taken and I need to take rest?"

'*Such a thought is purely fear based, my friend; you will come to understand that it cannot happen here. It is the prevalent way of thinking in your world, and you are still shrouded with it. Trust, if you need something, it is always available to you. Such is the nature of this world. It is also the nature of your world. However, prominent fear-based thinking has caused an overriding mentality of hoarding by a vast majority of people which has resulted in a serious lack for others. There has always been enough abundance on Earth to successfully sustain all of the people in your world, yet when fearful people store and stockpile rather than allowing to flow freely, the energy stagnates and you have some people with much, and others with little. This was never the plan.*'

At Sol's bidding, he ventured off on his own. The only instruction he was given before doing so was to allow his heart to guide him. He was so much closer to it in the silence of this world than he was in the noise of his own, and hearing what it had to tell him would be relatively easy. Sol mentioned that they would come back together soon, but until then he was to learn what he could from the world around him, as it had much to teach.

He no longer felt the deep fatigue within that he had felt earlier as he made his way to a grassy spot next to the falls and sat down. He definitely didn't want or need the rest in that moment, but he was guided by his heart to stay quiet for some time. This was a process similar to one that he remembered from what felt like lifetimes ago, when he used to head to the Vipassana meditation center not too far from where he grew up. Upon arriving, students would have to go to the main Gompa and sit in meditation for an hour to purge themselves of any dense energies they brought with them in order to allow the sacred space to remain light. It was not instructed to him by Sol upon arriving, but it just felt right for him to do so.

As he sat quietly in the grassy area observing the world around him, he noticed with a sense of curiosity that although the place had that distinct feeling any place has when it is being occupied by others, he could not actually physically see or hear anyone else. He was alone, yet certainly didn't feel that way.

After his quiet time adjusting to this vibrationally sensitive place, he slowly climbed to his feet and stepped from the grassy area onto a stone pathway. Immediately he was greeted by one of those whom he felt the presence of earlier yet could not see; a being similar to Sol, yet one that was distinctly feminine. Something he first observed in his guide without realizing it, and then consciously in this new being, was that it was difficult to focus on them the way one would when talking to another human back in his own world. They seemed human, yet also distinctly other worldly.

'Hello. My name is Mara. I noticed that you have observed, while spending time in the soft areas, that you cannot see or interact with any others. This is so that during the times you take rest, there is nothing but the beat of your own heart... no sounds, no distractions. You may have also noticed that the illumination in everything softened.'

"I did notice these things. It was almost as if the entire world went soft when I stepped into the circle of grass, as if everything went quiet so I could better focus. Speaking of which, why am I finding it so difficult to focus on you?"

She smiled: *'The act of truly being present with another being renders it almost impossible to judge what you are seeing in their "physical appearance." You will learn as your time here unfolds that the clarity in our appearance actually has nothing to do with your eyes, and everything to do with your heart. Because of the unique energetic properties of our world, and the lack of judgement that your world is currently full of, you will find that you don't truly "see" someone until you are interacting with them. You may also recognize a crude form of this from your own world in your encounters with various people; some of which you are immediately attracted to, and others you are not.'*

As she delivered her words directly into his mind, the definition in her appearance started becoming sharper to him and he could see that she possessed incredible beauty. Although she was shorter than Sol, she was definitely still much taller than he was. She had perfectly straight dark hair that hung to her waist, high cheek bones and fine features. Her body was slender yet portrayed a power that he had rarely seen before.

"Will you be one of my guides here?"

She spoke out loud to him with a very melodic voice. "Everyone here is going to guide you. We will all teach you things in different ways. Much the same way that everyone in your world can guide you if you are open and receptive to the lessons. Your only responsibility is to remain open enough to hear what we have to teach, and to allow yourself the space to truly know it for yourself."

Suddenly, her face broke into a mischievous smile. "Since we're using our voices, I'm going to let you in on a little secret of mine," she smiled at him as she continued. "Unlike most of the others here, I really enjoy using my voice to speak. Although it is completely unnecessary, I enjoy it for nothing more than the sake of it. Much like eating chocolate. I know I like chocolate, but I will still eat it at times because knowing you enjoy something is not the same as *actually* enjoying it."

He immediately understood where she was coming from. He had often had this very same discussion with people in his life. Those things that never need be spoken, he often enjoyed speaking because he just plain liked the taste of the words in his mouth.

"So, when do I begin my training here?" he asked verbally so as to indulge his host's desire for words.

"You already have, my friend," she said with another smile. "Observe all you can while you are here. This place is a true reflection of what your world has the potential to be."

She then stepped off gracefully and left him standing at the edge of the pool beside the falls.

CHAPTER 7

The Universal Principles

"The lips of wisdom are closed except to the ears of understanding."
The Kybalion

He spent what he roughly guessed could be about a week since his encounter with Mara beside the falls, wandering, exploring, resting, meditating, and generally enjoying the profound energy of the world he found himself in. Not sleeping was a very curious thing to him, but without cycles of day and night, without a discernible passage of time, he didn't grow tired. There was nothing but the moment, and the moment was always clear, vibrant, and perfect.

During that time, he came across maybe a dozen others that he spoke with at various lengths about different topics. They all knew him and he came to learn that they didn't just communicate via their minds; they had actually developed a true collective consciousness. What one of them knew, they all knew. Knowledge, wisdom, thought, and understanding were all shared with one another as if their minds were all plugged into a giant database and they all had permanent access to it.

He was walking slowly through a pristine grove of trees when Sol appeared to him, almost out of nowhere.

'I need you to come with me. There is something I have to tell you.'

He followed his guide into a clearing and down a path until they were standing at the base of the falls. Sol took his clothes off and stepped down into the hot water of the pool, beckoning him to do the same. As the water engulfed his naked body, he had a flashback to his dream which seemed as if it was a lifetime ago. He found it next to impossible to believe that he only left L.A. last night.

'All water is very much alive. Yet, the water of these falls, just like everything else here in our magical little world, loves to serve our highest good. What we are going to do now is have a conversation. Because of the energetic nature of the water that is currently permeating our cells, the impact of what we are about to speak of will be exponentially greater than it would be otherwise. With such potentially challenging concepts as the ones we are going to speak about, being immersed in this water will help you to understand. From now on all of our official lessons will take place here in these pools.'

"Lessons? This place is amazing, Sol, and I'm really loving my time here, but what is it that I am actually here to learn? You also told me that I would be the last to be taught this wisdom, and I still don't know what that means."

'Many years ago, in the world you have just come from, I was born and spent a single lifetime as the incarnation of a man known as "Thrice Great" Hermes Trismegistus. He was worshipped as Thoth, a God of great Wisdom. He was also the Father of Alchemy, giving these powerful tools to the inhabitants of the Earth. Part of what was given to the Human

race were seven Universal Principles by which to understand their place in the world. Hermes understood these Principles so well that he was able to engrave them onto the surface of an emerald - you may have heard it referred to as the Emerald Tablet. Such a thing could not have been achieved without a perfect and absolute understanding at the most fundamental level.

Although various Ascended Masters and Beings of immense energy have returned to Earth repeatedly across the ages to reawaken the thirst for such wisdom in humanity, most humans have turned a deaf ear to it, and those that did listen tried to grab at it, possess it, and twist it for their own selfish ends.

What you will come to know during your time here, my friend, is a complete understanding of these seven Universal Principles, and when your journey with us is done, you will leave here a Master Alchemist, able to share this wisdom with your own race for the highest good of all.

The first thing I want you to know is that you, me, this entire world, and thousands of Universes that sit unseen all around us are nothing more than a dream.'

And then Sol spoke these last words out loud: "THE ALL IS MIND. The Universe is Mental."

"What does that even mean, Sol? The Universe is Mental?" he asked verbally with a real look of confusion on his face.

'It means that the Universe and everything in it is mind. The ALL, God, Grace, Source, The Almighty IS, whatever term you desire, has created the Universe as a projection of its own Divine mind. As The ALL is in everything, and everything is in The ALL, there is nothing but The ALL. This being the case, there are no raw materials lying around outside of The ALL for it to "build" a Universe with.

Because the physical Universe follows patterns of birth, life, decline, death, and decay, it can clearly be stated that it is therefore different to the nature of God. God has no beginning and no ending. God does not work in cycles the same way that the physical Universe does. Aspects of the physical Universe can be defined and labeled whereas God sits beyond label or definition. These simple facts alone tell us without any doubt that

God and the Universe are not the same. Still, God created the Universe and everything in it in "His" image, and yet had no raw materials to "build with" outside of "Himself."

Science has long since proven that energy cannot be created or destroyed, only changed. If it exists, it has always existed, and if it doesn't exist, it never will. As something is unable to come from nothing, and by our very nature we are different to God, from what could THE ALL have created the Universe?

Similarly, if The ALL was to split a part of itself off from itself in order to create, that part would no longer be The ALL. This creates an impossible scenario since everything is God and God is everything. Having completely explored all of these potentialities, the only viable way remaining to create a Universe is the same way that we would create something if we were locked in a room with no materials for building and unable to replicate ourselves—as a projection of the mind.

THE ALL creates in its Infinite Mind countless Universes, which exist for eons of Time—and yet, to THE ALL, the creation, development, decline, and death of a million Universes is as long as the twinkling of an eye.'

He started to turn a little pale at what he was hearing. "Um, Sol? I'm feeling a little off right now. I think I'm going to need a little time to process this. I have never thought that I am really nothing more than a dream."

'Remember that time does not exist in this place. It is important for you to sit with this first Principle for as long as you need to, until your understanding of it is complete because understanding the remaining six Principles will all hinge on your understanding of this one.'

With that, Sol stepped from the pool, donned his robe, and vanished.

Because there were no cycles to measure time, he was unsure how long he had been contemplating what Sol had referred to as the first Universal Principle. As he moved silently through the amazing world he was currently in, he tried to imagine everything he was interacting with as just a dream, and because everything was so vastly different to "his world," it really wasn't that difficult for him to do so.

"Don't think of it as 'just a dream,'" he heard words spoken out loud for the first time in what felt like ages to him. He turned around from where he was contemplating a fruit tree bearing some amazingly large, ripe apples to see Mara standing behind him, smiling.

"When you try to perceive it as 'just a dream,' you take away from the power that is contained within dreams, and you will never fully appreciate or understand the Principle, or dreams."

"I don't understand. I mean, when we dream it is brief, and doesn't mean anything to our real life once we're awake."

"Exactly", replied Mara while grinning from ear to ear. "Now you're starting to get it."

With that, she took a bite from an apple she had plucked from the fruit tree, started humming a funny little tune, and walked away.

He found himself relaxing in the pools of the falls, not really thinking about any ideas or dreams, or trying to understand unusual concepts, but just allowing things to be, as they were. In whatever time had passed since his lesson with Sol, he had nearly sent himself crazy trying to envision the world and himself as a dream. Everything is so solid and "real," how could this be a dream? In some way, allowing his mind to relax and not strain to comprehend things, allowed the wisdom of the first Universal Principle to completely permeate into him; in not trying to understand it, he completely understood it.

'What took you so long? I have been waiting for you', said Sol's smiling voice from within his mind. His guide once again appeared from out of nowhere, stripped off his robe, and climbed down into the water with him.

"Sorry it took me so long. That was a real challenge."

'In reality, it actually only took but a single moment, my friend. You are so new here that your mind still tries to grasp at the passage of time in the way your world has programmed you to think of it; that is, at the concept of time being linear; it is not. To us, there truly is no time. This is also yet another example of the mental nature of the Universe. This world is at a much higher vibration than yours. Therefore, it is a great deal closer

to the truth of reality. Here there are less illusions attempting to block you from the truth of all things.'

"I understand. Dreams are powerful by and of their very nature, as is imagination. Accordingly, we have the ability to be or do anything we desire. It is only because the Universe is a mental projection of The All that we can actually experience "life" in the way that we do."

'Very profound understanding, my friend. This leads us right to the second Universal Principle, which is the Principle of Correspondence. I'm certain that you have heard the axiom, 'As above, so below; as below, So Above.' According to the Principle of Correspondence, whatever is possible on one level must therefore be possible on all levels. This Principle exists because there are actually not different and separate planes of energy, but only one that is divided by nothing more than degree of vibration.'

"That actually makes complete sense to me for some reason, Sol."

'I'm not surprised. We have been watching the work you have done in coming to grips with the first Principle. That has laid a very solid foundation for you in understanding the remaining six.

What you need to know is that in regards to the possibility of something being able to happen, plausibility does not come into it; if it is possible to the Divine mind of The ALL, then it is possible on all of the levels created by the mind of The ALL, because all levels or planes are actually the same. Therefore, if you can imagine something, it can exist. It is this understanding that also gives birth to one of the most interesting elements of life—The Law of Paradox.

Just because something is possible does not mean it will ever happen. The perceived limitations of the world in which we live are vastly different to the limitations on higher levels of "reality." It is because we perceive any limitations at all that we further reinforce and perpetuate our limited perceptions, thus narrowing our field of view of what is possible. In this way we continue to create so many strong limitations in our lives that otherwise would not be there. As such we may never permit ourselves the space to expand enough in full comprehension of the possibility of something, regardless of whether it actually IS possible or not.

Your fields of science are finally starting to align with this Universal Principle via Quantum Mechanics, and the understanding that we create our own reality with our mind is now a fact that has been proven. The fact that this aspect of our various realities is constantly being proven time and again also adds credibility to the Principle of Mentalism. As Above, so below; as below, So Above. If we can do it, The ALL can do it, and if The ALL can do it, then we can do it.'

"But Sol, isn't this potentially a very egotistical statement, comparing the nature of ourselves and what we are capable of to that of God?"

'My friend, when you dream, is it fair to say that what you dream about is actually in no way different to you? That if you are able to run a marathon in 'reality' and you were to then dream a version of yourself that could run a marathon, that somehow the dream creation of yourself is being egotistical because it can do what you are capable of? Instead of thinking about it in such a manner and using limited beliefs to understand the point, allow it to expand you to an understanding on the connection between God, the Universe, and yourself! In pursuing such a thought pattern with an open and loving mind, you will come to realize that you truly are a part of the Divine ALL, albeit as a projection of Mind.

For our purposes there are only three recognized Great Planes of reality: the Physical, the Mental, and the Spiritual. These are divided in seven minor planes, which are further divided into another seven sub-planes. All of the degrees of Life within the Universe fall into the dimensions, and it is worthy of noting that the dimensional divisions are purely arbitrary; they are all one, and they fade into each other. They exist in any discernible separation only by degree of vibration. What I want you to do is explain that to me in your own way. As the last true Alchemist to purvey this wisdom to the inhabitants of Earth, you will need to know how to explain it to other people in a very efficient manner. Begin with me...'

He hesitated briefly before speaking. "OK, so there are three planes of reality, separated into numerous sub-planes, but instead of thinking about it as separate or different energies that make up these different planes, it's all one energy and the only thing that makes the "reality" of the planes different, is the speed at which the energy vibrates... And regardless of the speed of vibration, they are ALL governed by the one set of Laws. How's that, Sol?"

'VERY good, my friend. You have understood this quickly. One of the key points that we need to take from The Principle of Correspondence is that the only differences we perceive as existing in the Universe are that of vibration alone, and this is why something that is possible on one level is possible on all levels. It is only with a complete understanding of this Principle that we obtain the "glue" which holds the remaining Principles in place for us. You have done this masterfully.

We are going to head to a different place now for your next lesson. We will still be making use of the intelligence of the water to speed your learning. However, we are going to make our way up the falls to the top pool.'

Although he had done a fair amount of rock climbing in his younger years, he felt a knot tighten in his stomach at the thought of having to climb a wet, slippery rock face. Glancing up the cascading water, he noted with a bite of fear that he couldn't even *see* where the top pool was, let alone imagine climbing all the way up there without ropes.

Sol's voice echoed gently in his mind:

'What would you choose to do if you knew you could not fail?'

He flashed back to his 9-year-old self, standing in front of his mother who had just handed him a card with the exact same quote written on it. He remembered thinking, at that time, he wouldn't attempt anything if he *knew* he couldn't fail, because it was only the fear of not achieving what he was chasing that made it so appealing.

'So, what happened to that, my friend?' asked Sol who was quietly observing his thought process. *'Is it still fear of failing, or falling as the case may be, that drives you? Has it also not been an immense fear of not truly living that has driven you time and again across your life into the dangerous places and situations that you have frequently encountered?'*

"I guess that when I fell into the rut my life had become, I moved away from all of that. I stopped *living* and chasing life. Everything became nothing more than the process and routine of life, without any real living occurring. I have been living only to perpetuate my life," he said as his shoulders slumped noticeably at the realization.

Sol stepped forward and grabbed his shoulders firmly with both hands. The tall man had a vice-like grip.

"NOW is the time to reawaken from that my friend."

The words came out audibly instead of through the mind connection and had a very powerful effect on him. In that instant, he reconnected with everything that he once was; he found himself standing on the edge of cliffs that he had just scaled. He was windsurfing across a stretch of ocean at 30 knots with the sea spray in his face thrusting him into the full glory of the moment... such moments that he had lived a thousand times over. Such moments all but forgotten because of the process of life that had ground him down. In that instant, he was surging like a raging ocean, roaring like a fire engulfing anything in its path. He was ALIVE!

"And now, we climb," Sol softly said to him.

Together they made their way from the waist-deep pool they had been standing in at the forest floor and slowly began their way up the falls. He noticed with slight amusement that even though the rocks were wet, they were not slippery. The feeling of the experience was quite different to climbing on a dry rock face, but certainly no more challenging. The other curious phenomenon that really stood out to him was produced by exerting himself in the perpetual moment of this strange world, yet without the flow of time to fatigue him.

In his younger years, he always used to toy with the concept that if one could stay in the moment completely while doing an activity such as rock climbing, one would exist perfectly without fear and beyond fatigue. When one finds oneself struggling with something, whether it be physical, mental, or emotional, it is purely the thought that what is currently being experienced will always be experienced. In recognizing that what we are experiencing is only being experienced in this moment, even if the next moment is exactly the same, it is still only the moment.

One moment led to another until they were finally standing on the top of the fall. Several times during the climb he had felt the touch of panic surround him as he struggled to find a line forward, yet each time he surprised himself with the ease at which he was able to sit with it and allow it to pass as the moment passed, rather than engage with it.

"How do you feel?" asked the now familiar voice of Mara from somewhere behind him. He turned slowly to see his friend lounging beside the pristine rock pool he and Sol had just climbed.

"I feel great. I guess I was right all those years ago about fear and fatigue existing only because we project it forward in time from the current moment..."

"You certainly were", she laughed. "And look how serious you took yourself all those times when you could have instead just been enjoying what was occurring."

"So, you made the climb earlier?" he asked her while sitting down on a rock between her and Sol.

"Goodness, no. There's a lovely forest trail that leads around behind the falls and winds its way up here. Although the climb is certainly exhilarating, I thoroughly enjoy the walk and, in many respects, it is even more rewarding with some of the encounters you have along the way. We can take the walk once your lessons up here are finished."

He looked at Sol who was observing a bright green dragonfly lightly kiss a tree branch next to where he was sitting.

"A trail, huh?"

'There is always more than one way of doing something, my friend. In many cases, there is a much easier path than the one we have chosen. However, in almost every single instance, when we choose the challenging path, it is because we need it. You needed that climb to completely reawaken to the most fundamental and primitive version of yourself. Everything that you are learning here with us would be gone from you before you arrived back at your tent in your own world if you had not made that connection to yourself.'

"I understand that, and thank you for pushing me."

'The other reason we made the climb is because you needed to completely feel and trust what you have always suspected to be the truth about fear, panic, and fatigue before we began the next lesson. Understanding

and knowing these things on an experiential level will make your grasp of the Principle of Vibration so much stronger.'

He laughed out loud, "I'm really starting to understand the difference between knowing something as a concept, and knowing it as an experience."

'Although it is always infinitely better to experientially know something rather than to merely intellectually know it, it is not always achievable from where we stand. When this happens, we must find a way to expand our position of understanding through experience. Hence, the reason we climbed the fall rather than took the trail up here.

Now, under Universal Law, and according to the Principle of Vibration, there is no such thing as matter. Everything that the inhabitants of your world once took as solid and unmoving has always been particles of energy vibrating at a very slow, dense rate. Your science has finally started catching up with this understanding.

The Principle of Vibration provides the framework of our Universe, allowing us the insight into the layers upon layers of energy, how emotion is more powerful than thought, how thought is more powerful than the physical reality, and how all of it is subject to the LAW. In understanding such a thing, we have the ability to move above dis-ease and actively create our reality by shifting the vibration from which we operate.

Alchemy gives us further insight, via this Principle, into the connection of everything in the Universe. Anything that we perceive as separate to anything else, including ourselves, is purely because it is vibrating at a different rate. I am nothing more than a direct reflection of you, my friend; it is only the degree of vibration that creates the illusion of separation. Mara, myself, the others you have encountered here, even this place itself, are all a part of you.

You see it all as separate because it is vibrating faster than you are. Ordinarily that would mean that you would not have the ability to see or interact with any of it. However, in this case your own energetic vibration has been altered upward so that you could come "here" and learn from "us."'

"Are you saying that I can see or interact with anything that vibrates at a slower rate than me, but not generally with anything that is vibrating faster than me? Is that correct?"

'Generally speaking. Of course, there are always exceptions, and it is these exceptions that have permitted Alchemists across the ages to perform what would be deemed 'miraculous' feats. When one has a complete understanding of Universal LAW, one can use higher to overcome lower. The Universal Principles are irrefutable and will always stand unbroken and unbreakable. That does not mean that they cannot be moved.

Think about the Principle of Correspondence and how it states that if something is possible on one level, it is possible on all levels. Everything that we can do here in this world, we can also do in your world. Yet, they would be looked upon as miracles because it is not "normal" for one to achieve such things in such a dense vibration.

This is also the reason that neither you nor we are able to comprehend the energy of God. When energy vibrates at a fast enough rate, it appears to be motionless. The reason that The ALL, or God, cannot be defined is purely because the degree of vibration emanating from IT is at such an infinite and intensely rapid rate that IT is perceived to be at complete rest. In a Universe where EVERYTHING vibrates, that which appears to be at complete rest will be deemed as "Nothingness" or void.'

Sol continued: *'The beauty that this Principle gives us is that we can find a connection with God if we make choices that take the high road. We can choose to act from a place of lower "egoic" self, which is largely ruled by fear, and thus create a low vibration, or we can choose to act from the place of love within ourselves, which facilitates and perpetuates a higher vibration.*

Take a moment to notice this next time you make a decision. Are you left feeling low, drained, or in doubt that you made the correct choice, or are you feeling enlivened, light, and free from what you chose? Sharing this understanding to other people is one of the most beautiful gifts you can give. If they never take this work any further, bringing this awareness into daily life and the multitude of decisions that are made has the power to increase one's connection to God.'

"Sol, all of this is making perfect sense to me. It is as if I have always known it, and you are just reminding me that I know it."

Sol's face lit up brighter than he had ever seen it: *'That is because you HAVE always known it all, my dear friend. Like I said, I am merely a mirror of you, so for "me" to be giving "you" these lessons means that you already know it all. We will never come to understand anything that we haven't already come to know.*

From here, my friend, you must take a short journey. Mara and I will wait for you to complete the next lesson. In order to learn and understand what comes next, you must take this journey alone.'

"What? You're not coming with me? But I thought you were my guide during my entire time here. How will I know where to go?" As he spoke, he noticed he was racing his words out with a little panic painted on them.

"I know you said I already know all of this, but I don't remember that I know it until you speak to me about it." He spoke out loud without consciously realizing it, and it was Mara rather than Sol that replied.

"My beautiful friend, part of your time here is to learn how to find the reflections you need to see in everything, not just from the voice of someone who speaks with you. When you know how to look, you can be taught by everything. If you are ever feeling stuck, calm yourself with your breath. This is your most powerful anchor back to yourself. When you have settled within, take a moment and look again. Be at peace now, take this journey, follow the signs and return to me when you have understood," she lightly kissed his forehead and then stepped away.

Sol's calming voice appeared back in his mind:

'Follow the river, my friend, and you will come to a place of immense power. Even for this world, where you are heading will stand out. You will know without a doubt when you have found what it is you seek. This sacred place has been created with unusual properties so that you will recognize cycles and feel the passage of time. Do not be concerned about this. It is an illusion created for a very specific purpose. Regardless of how long you are there, time itself is still nonexistent for all intents and purposes. Now, follow the river...'

Follow the River

"The river always flows.
Whether you choose to remain in
The Flow or not is entirely up to you."
WARRIOR.PHILOSOPHICAL

He set off with a little trepidation from the top pool of the falls and walked alongside the river. The first thing he started noticing was that the lushness of the forest soon gave way once again to a stark and rugged beauty of ice and rock. Although the hot water of the river still snaked across the terrain, it had not created a warm, tropical forest like it had around the falls. As he kept walking, he also noticed that the light was starting to become a little less bright. It was still coming from within everything rather than overhead like a sun would produce, but it was definitely less vibrant than it had been back at the rock pool.

Nestled in amongst the rocks were bright little flowers of different colors. They took advantage of the water to sustain their life, growing mostly along the banks of the river. At first, he didn't pay much attention to them, focusing instead on rushing towards a destination that he was told he would immediately recognize. As he walked, however, he noticed that the little flowers kept catching his focus for some unknown reason, so he took a moment to stop and sit quietly.

He closed his eyes and started focusing on his breath, following the air as it flowed in and out of his lungs. As he started to become more still in his practice, he noticed something most unusual about the flowers. The reason that they had kept catching his eye was because they were actually observing him. They didn't just start to glow more brightly; they actually grew taller in his direction as if reaching towards him. He smiled as he reached his hand out towards one which in turn reached its petals towards his hand and when they connected, he was immediately thrust into a sacred space of deep knowing.

It was as if the history of the entire world he found himself in was recorded within the flower's cellular memory, and it wanted to share with him. By the end of the encounter, he had tears streaming down his cheeks. He had just experienced a more significant connection with a little flower growing in amongst some rocks along a river bank than he had had with most people across his entire life.

He sat for a while longer immersed in the beauty of the moment before finally getting to his feet. As he progressed further up the river, he eventually started to notice that it was almost twilight. Just as the light started to completely give way to an ensuing darkness, he came to a fork in the river.

'Sol, you never mentioned anything about a fork...' he caught the thought and stopped it before it went any further. As he cut the thought off, Sol's voice echoed back to him.

'You will know without a doubt when you have found what it is you seek.'

He decided to sit for a few moments and take stock. What happens now? He was in a strange place without his guide, and he had once again become subject to the cycles of time, although Sol had told him that it was just an illusion. Wasn't all time just an illusion? Illusion or not, it still had the ability to harm him. After-all, he had learned recently that the entire Universe was a daydream of God, yet he also realized that despite the illusory nature of the world, he could not tell his landlord that he was no longer paying rent because he was nothing more than a dream.

Somehow this approach to every aspect of life would simply not work, because hunger, homelessness and destitution were all very real. There are consequences to actions, and despite the nature of the world in which he both came from, and currently found himself, he knew he must act accordingly.

A voice he had not yet known echoed in his mind: *'This is indeed a very heavy paradox, because what you are perceiving is not "real" yet needs to be treated as such in order to make any progression up the energetic spectrum.'*

"Who said that?" he asked out loud.

The voice came back again: *'Stand up!'*

It was so compelling that he was on his feet before he knew what was happening.

'Where do I go? Which river do I follow?' he thought the words and noticed that there was a little trepidation in them. No answer.

Looking around in the failing light, he saw a cave directly upstream between the fork of the two rivers. Despite the darkness, the mouth of the cave still appeared slightly more illuminated.

Mara's voice reverberated across his mind: *'Follow the signs.'*

With that, he waded into the water and crossed the branch of the river to make his way to the cave.

For the first time since arriving in this world, he felt tired. The strenuous physical exertion had really started weighing on him. When he entered the mouth of the cave, he gratefully slumped to the ground, leaned against a rock, and almost immediately drifted off into a deep sleep.

When he finally opened his eyes, it was early morning. He had always liked this time of day, because it was much earlier than most people wanted to be awake, and it had always represented potential to him. It was the time of day that brought with it the blank canvas on which all new beginnings were painted. Lovers that had fallen asleep angry with one another could embrace and forgive. Hostilities spoken the day before could be left where they had been spoken. Yes, if there was ever a time for new beginnings, it was the dawn of day.

He quickly realized as the world around him started becoming lighter that even the darker reaches of the cave were beginning to vibrate with light. Daybreak in this place seemed to mean that there was zero darkness. Because the light didn't come from a single point above, there were no shadows, no hidden places where the light was unable to penetrate and shine. Although it seemed unusual to him at first, it also made complete sense. He felt as though night should be completely dark, and day should be completely light. This was the perfect way to balance the cycles and perpetuate harmony. The way it was meant to be.

A brief glance around the inside of the cave and he found that the walls were covered in all manner of symbols, glyphs, and writings etched into the rock. Just as the symbols from his dream, some he recognized, some he did not. After exploring the carvings with his eyes, he came to rest on a phrase that was etched above all else in the back corner of the cave:

~So, we need not dwell upon the feature of illusion. Rather let us, in recognizing the real nature of the Universe, seek to understand its mental laws, and endeavor to use them to the best effect in our upward progress through life...~ Kybalion

He had no idea what Kybalion was, but the wisdom sat well within him.

'The Kybalion is an ancient text from your world in which the Hermetic Alchemists kept record of the seven Universal Principles.'

The voice was in his mind just like it had been with Sol and Mara, yet it had a different quality to it. It was as if it didn't just come from a single point, spoken from the mind of one other person. Rather, it was as if the walls of the cave itself were vibrating the words into his mind.

"Who are you? Why can I not see you?"

'Because you are not looking with your heart', the voice replied with a power he had never known. If the voice had told him to walk back to the falls and jump off, he felt that he somehow wouldn't have much choice in the matter.

"Are you another guide like Sol?"

'Not like Sol. He has had reason to remain in physical form at this stage. I chose to remain in the collective conscious; I no longer had a need for the body I inhabited.'

"So, you are just *there?*"

'If you wish to know me and further expand your understanding of Truth, stop trying to wrap your intellectual mind around it. Such things will only ever be met with failure. Close your eyes, forget your mind, and look with your heart.'

He did as he was told, and after a few moments he started to feel that there was an intelligence within the rocks themselves. The light that was now illuminating the cave and vibrating brightly out of all things was actually alive and speaking to him directly. He also realized that it wasn't a single person's consciousness at all with which he was communicating. It was the collective of Sol's entire race that had gone beyond the need of a body. Each time one of the race passed, they would join into this collective. This was why the voice had so much power and authority... it contained the energy of many souls.

'Very good. You are to remain as my guest now for some time. I will challenge you, and force you to look at things more deeply than you have ever done so. Your time with me will not be comfortable, however that is by design. Comfort zones are beautiful places, but nothing grows within them. YOU, growing to experientially understand the Universal Principles of the Hermetics so that you may give the wisdom to the others of your world, is the only thing that will save it.'

"I thought that according to the first three Universal Principles, we could use Law against Law, higher against lower to achieve all kinds of miraculous things. My world is not real! Why am I the only one that can save it? I don't understand," he said.

The voice was still calm, yet firm with an unwavering intensity, *'Because your race has forgotten itself and the truth of its own nature. You are believing your own illusionary creations. As a race, you have come to believe that everything is real, solid and unchangeable, however in doing so you refuse to acknowledge what you cannot see. Alternatively, if the wisdom of the Hermetics was delivered incorrectly and taken the wrong way, it would have disastrous consequences.*

By acting as though nothing is real, we will then also act as though the Principles and Laws which govern our realities are not real. The issue with this approach is that they ARE irrefutable. In believing that our life is but a dream, we can jump off a cliff and despite our beliefs, we will still die. These Principles and Laws govern every aspect of our existence, whether we acknowledge them or not, however it is only in acknowledging that the Universe is real to us that the Principles and Laws become real to us too. When something is real, we then gain power in our ability to work with it and mold it.

We are made of the exact same substance that the governing Laws are made from, even if it is nothing more than a projection of God's mind. Therefore, by embracing the Laws rather than ignoring them, we embrace our truth and gain mastery over ourselves, and the Laws.'

He calmed himself and prompted the voice to continue.

'The half-wise, recognizing the comparative unreality of the Universe, imagine that they may defy its Laws. They are vain and presumptuous fools, and they are broken against the rocks, torn asunder by reason of their folly. The truly wise, knowing the nature of the Universe, use Law against laws; the higher against the lower; and by the Art of Alchemy transmute that which is undesirable into that which is worthy, and thus triumph. Mastery consists not in abnormal dreams, visions, and fantastic imaginings or living, but in using the higher forces against the lower — escaping

the pains of the lower planes by vibrating on the higher. Transmutation, not presumptuous denial, is the weapon of the Master.'

"What you're essentially telling me is that if you ignore the principles, or recognize them however believe that the Laws are breakable, then your life will become miserable because they are still governing you and you are unable to do anything about it?"

'That is correct. More often than not, it is when people live in this state that creates the majority of suffering in the world. Go outside of the cave and sit in between the confluence of the rivers. Observe and return only when you can tell me why I have sent you there.'

He got up without another word and moved to the tip of the "V" in the space of dry land where the two rivers became one. He found a rock to perch on and made himself as comfortable as he could. Looking around, he noticed that one river flowed a little faster than the other, yet as the two waters met they blended into the same speed. He sat for hours staring at the water swirling and eddying as two rivers became one and continued their journey down to the top of the falls. He found his thoughts drifting to Mara, wondering what she was doing, and for the briefest flicker of a moment, he felt a smile appear in his mind.

Although he was unsure of why he was tasked with sitting and watching the rivers converge, eventually he started to recognize that there was a pattern emerging in the world around him. The two rivers that merged both contained the same water; although their journeys to arrive at this point were unknown and potentially vastly different, they were ultimately the same.

Just as he had that last thought, he was hit with a blinding white light that knocked him to the flat of his back. In an instant, he felt the crown of his head burning with an intensity he had never known, and the words came into his mind: *'Everything is Dual. Everything has poles. Everything has its pair of opposites. Like and unlike are the same. Opposites are identical in nature, but different in degree. Extremes meet. All truths are but half-truths. All paradoxes may be reconciled.'*

Without any further prompting, he stood up, turned, and walked back to the cave. The light was already fading as he made his way to the spot where he had slept the night before, and he realized that he had been beside the river for hours.

The voice that had sent him to the river earlier came back to him: *'It was important for you to come to this place for a very simple reason... It is here and here alone in this world that you have the ability to observe the Principle of Polarity in motion.'*

"You mean because of the two rivers being one?"

'Partially, yes. The endless flow of the river enabled you to have the realization you had. It is also because this place and its immediate surroundings are subject to cycles of time that the rest of this world is not. Day and night are not separate. Regardless of how well you remember them from your world, you needed to feel this cycle with your new understanding to be in a state of experiential awareness before you leave here.'

"That makes perfect sense," he replied.

The energy of the Elders continued: *'The Principle of Polarity shows us that the things we once took as being separate and unrelated are actually one. Working with this Universal Principle starts to show us that elements such as hot and cold are not two separate things. They are actually the same, separated by nothing other than degree; we refer to it as temperature, and both 'hot' and 'cold' are but different aspects of the same thing.'*

"How does this actually apply to me in life though? I mean, knowing that hot and cold are ultimately the same thing is a very profound understanding to come to, but how do I actually make use of it to improve things for myself and others?"

'Because of the Principle of Correspondence and the axiom, "As Above, so below; as below, So Above," you came to understand that whatever is possible on one level is possible on all levels. If something on the physical level, such as thermal dynamics, encompassing both hot and cold as the one thing separated by degree of temperature only, then the same is true of emotions. Love and hate are the same thing, separated only by the degree of vibration they exhibit.'

At that moment he felt as though he had been slapped on the forehead by a giant cosmic hand. The simplicity of what he had just come to know was mind-blowing. His mind reached back into various memories over his entire life, and as he recalled times of elation and heartbreak, victory and loss, happiness and sadness, he *felt* the choice to change it from one to the other had always been there.

The Elders continued: *'You are correct. Every step of the way there has been a choice... there always will be. The reason this Principle is so important to us is because it shows us that we have the power to change what we feel in any given moment by changing the vibration of our thoughts and emotions. We have the ability to shift a thought from anger to calm, and the ability to shift an emotion from hate to love as readily as we can turn hot water into ice. Imagine exhibiting a level of self-control so empowered, that when you are knocked down by an aspect of life, you get to choose what happens within you, within your mental state, and within your emotional responses. Imagine being able to do it as easily as the flow of day to night. The true power of Alchemical Transmutation was in turning Hate into Love, not lead into gold.'*

Just like everything he had learned since arriving in this unusual world, he acknowledged within himself that he already knew what he was learning.

'Although it is very important to be mindful of your thoughts, it is even more important to be mindful of how you feel about your thoughts. Every single thought, emotion, and mental state has its own degree of vibration, which will either keep you up or bring you down. Although such things are governed by the Principle of Vibration, the will of a consciously empowered Human is stronger than the Principle.

The Principle always exists. That is irrefutable. However, this doesn't mean it cannot be worked with and manipulated. When you make an active choice in your life, what you are choosing is nothing more than which vibrationary rate to exhibit, rather than allowing yourself to remain sitting in a particular vibration due to the circumstance in which you have found yourself. You are choosing your vibration, rather than having it chosen for you.'

The voice of the collective energy paused for a moment, and he felt that it was waiting for him. When he spoke, it was out loud and in a very reflective manner.

"I have always lived my life according to cycles. Things have always come and gone. There have been moments that I have found favorable, and those I have found abhorrent. I recognize now that I have allowed myself to remain a victim of circumstance, by finding myself happy when my situation has been favorable and unhappy when it wasn't.

However, I can see with so much clarity now in realizing that despite what happens outside of myself, I still have the power to choose my response, *then* I am using Law against Law to create a favorable outcome. The time I was accused of ruining my Mother's life, I truly did have the power to see myself how I wanted rather than allowing the external situation to make me a victim".

He felt the voice smile for the first time since he arrived at the cave.

'THIS is the true power of Alchemy within your life! Forget the dusty old chambers, and how to create gold from lead. The real transformational power of this miraculous Art is in your ability to create gold within yourself and your own life, from the base materials you have to begin with.'

CHAPTER 9

The Lessons ARE the journey

"The Obstacle IS the Path."
Zen Proverb

Four days had passed since he arrived at the cave, and he had been in the relative silence of an almost meditative state throughout that entire time. Periodically, when he had a question about his understandings, the voice of the Elders would challenge him with further questions to facilitate the growth of his answers.

He also went back over his entire life, memory by memory and changed the way he perceived what had happened. Each time he did this, he felt a little lighter. The interesting thing he noted was that at no point did his ability to change his past require apologies or forgiveness from anyone else. It was ALL in his own hands, and he realized that it always had been.

The light was fading as he sat beside one of the rivers in a little spot that he had come to love, his feet dangling into the hot water. He wasn't exactly sure what it was about that spot in particular, but it seemed to sing for him whenever he sat there. Suddenly his mind became abuzz with words from the Elders: *'Everything flows, out and in; everything has its tides; all things rise and fall; the pendulum-swing manifests in everything; the measure of the swing to the right is the measure of the swing to the left; rhythm compensates.'*

Nothing further was said, and he found himself full of questions. As darkness descended upon him, he lay back and gazed up at a night sky ablaze with stars. What a truly beautiful place he had found. How would he ever manage to bring himself to leave such an amazing world and return to the one that he came from? With that thought, he drifted off into a deep, peaceful sleep.

Throughout the night he experienced many strange yet profound dreams. For a brief time, he was an ocean, a giant body of saline water, deep and mysterious, stretching across the surface of the planet. He could feel the rise and fall of his own powerful tides against the various rocks, cliffs, and beaches of the world. He felt himself warming as the great sun above shone down upon his vast body during the day, and cooling as the night air danced across his surface. Although he didn't consciously understand, he instinctively knew that the cycles of the moon above him somehow affected his own cycles.

He dreamt that he was a mountain standing tall and proud over the plains below. During the cold winter months, he was covered in snow and ice, yet during summer he was ablaze with wildflowers, long grass, and life. Such cycles of weather played deeply important roles in his interaction with the world around him.

He awoke to the voice of the Elders once again sounding inside his mind: '*The fifth Great Universal Principle shows us the nature of the Flow. Our entire Universe is governed by Rhythm; tides rise and fall, day becomes night which becomes day again. The force of Rhythm manifests between the poles that the Principle of Polarity defined for us. Absolutely everything that exists, both seen and unseen, does so within the spectrum of the poles and rides the pendulum to a greater or lesser degree.*'

"That explains the dreams I had last night about all of the cycles," he replied.

'*Indeed. Once again, you needed to feel such a thing in order to completely understand it.*

Because of the nature of The Principle of Rhythm, the further something swings one way, the further it will swing to the opposite. By Law of the Principle, when something swings to the right, it must come back to the left at an exactly equal and opposite force.

We see this in nature all the time as you experienced in your dreams; extremely high tides are followed by extremely low tides; harsh winters are followed by long summers, yet we also see it in our own emotions. As an example, in your everyday life, how often have you felt a little down, only to then find that the very next day is fantastic? How often have you struggled through some major hardship in life, and then had a major breakthrough and achieved something wonderful? This is the Principle of Rhythm at work, and the key to it is this: Although you cannot stop the pendulum from swinging, you do have the choice at any point to polarize yourself where you desire.

The pendulum is always swinging back and forth, because it is an integral part of the great fabric of our reality. Yet, focused Human will is stronger than the Principle, and through force of our conscious will we can move above it, and allow ourselves to stay where we desire without having to swing back to the opposite side again. This place below the falls is a perfect example of such a thing. Despite the frigid mountain air, the ice and the rocks all about, it remains energetically centered within its own climate.'

"How do I actually do it - polarize myself where I desire so that I don't ride the pendulum?"

The actual process of polarizing yourself at the point which you desire is done by choice. Yet you must be aware of the fact that you have a choice, so the first step is awareness. Your choice is then reinforced with a laser-like focus backed up with a powerful will, this is all about action. Finally, the process is completed with the total surrender of acceptance.

"So, it's about using my mind to force and hold myself where I want to be?"

No! Although this process sounds like hard mental work that requires some manner of brute force, it truly only comes from a place of acceptance. How can you force yourself to be genuinely happy? You can only force an act of happiness, never the real thing. How do you use brute force to maintain anything in life without eventually fatiguing yourself? You cannot. Despite what happens outside of yourself, you always have the choice to observe the way the pendulum swings your emotions, and actively make the choice not to engage with that motion. You only ever achieve this by surrendering, never forcing.

"I think I understand," he replied. "When something in life happens that I don't like, I can stay above the swing of the pendulum in a two-fold manner; in surrendering to the process of the situation rather than trying to control it, and choosing my emotional response to it rather than being swept along and blindly reacting to it."

Very good. But also remember that it doesn't just have to be a reaction to a thing you don't like that puts you back onto the pendulum. A situation that you find joy in can do the same thing if you attach to it and try to control it by holding onto it; if you then allow your joy to be a blind reaction rather than a choice, you are back on that pendulum and the further you swing to the left, the further you will swing to the right.

CHAPTER 10

The Desert of Humanity

"One's destination is never a place,
but a new way of seeing things."
Henry Miller

He awoke one morning in the cave and had the realization that the consciousness of the Elders had taught him everything they needed to teach. It had been approximately a month since the day he arrived, and the Elders had shown him an entirely new way of looking at his life; they had also helped him to gain an even greater understanding of the first three Universal Principles.

One conversation with the Elders had stood out for him above all the others. He was concerned that although he had gained a beautiful new way of perceiving the world, he was also deeply marred by his past and the journey that he had walked to arrive here had left him unable to change particular patterns.

"What is the point in having so much empowerment in life if I am still reactive because of my previous conditionings?"

'Something you will learn in great detail with the next Universal Principle is that your ability to make changes to your path does not just stretch forward. Such thinking is a trap that one would fall into when one only understands time as linear. Because time does not exist, it is just as easy for you to change the events that have already come to pass as it is to change what hasn't happened yet.'

"So, I can change the past? That's not something they teach you about in school," he said with sarcasm in his voice.

'You can change what has "happened" to you by changing the way you see it. If you think back to your understanding of the Universal Principles that you've learned so far, you can see how the way you perceive an event changes the very event itself. This is not specific to what is currently happening around you. Think about a time when you were a child and something happened that you thought was "bad."'

The time that he had started having panic attacks sprung to mind. He was 16 and it was the accumulation of a mountain worth of stress in his life. It also heralded one of the most significant turning points in his life. There was so much happening around him that he was taking on as his own, things that didn't belong to him; there was so much he was taking personally and couldn't properly deal with, and it finally accumulated as an overload of anxiety.

At the time he hated his life. He feared the next panic attack, and he was generally miserable with the circumstances around him.

'Instead of using those experiences to justify your actions today, look at what happened and send love to the experience. Know that it wasn't by accident yet rather a deliberate set of circumstances that created an exact

event to help teach you a powerful lesson. Find and embrace your lesson in it and you have changed the past.'

He came back to the moment, feeling the hard rock floor of the cave beneath him. When he realized that the Elders were no longer communicating with him, he knew in his heart that it was time to head back to Sol. Realizing that there was no rush, he sat by the convergence of the two rivers in his special little spot enjoying the quiet stillness for another couple of hours, watching the bright dragonflies hovering over the water before slowly climbing to his feet and commencing his journey down the river.

As he walked, his mind was strangely calm. He found himself in a state of complete stillness and was just observing the nature of things around him. Although the terrain he was walking over didn't look familiar to him, he wasn't concerned. It had been at least a month since he had walked up from the top of the falls.

It wasn't long before he came to another fork in the river. How had he not noticed this on the way up? Surely he would have seen another branch of the river, as large as the main flow heading off in another direction. He stood at this new junction for some time, weighing which river to take in order to return to the falls.

Once again Mara's words echoed in his mind: *Follow the signs... If you are ever feeling stuck, calm yourself with your breath and when you have settled within, look again.*

He sat down cross legged at the new fork, closed his eyes, and focused on his breathing. His mind tried to stray a couple of times toward fearful thoughts of becoming perpetually lost in a world where time didn't exist. He wondered briefly what would happen to him if he couldn't find his way back. Was Sol or Mara or even the Elders within a close enough distance to hear his cries for help? Would he end up wandering forever in this strange landscape? After a few moments of straying thoughts, he brought his mind back to his breath, and was finally able to settle within himself.

When he opened his eyes again, he found that the river branch to the left seemed to be a little brighter than the one to the right, just as the cave mouth had appeared to be when he first arrived at the junction up-stream. After taking in the scenery for a few moments, he closed his eyes again and went back within, focusing his thoughts into the brighter left branch of the river.

He flowed along on a gentle stream of mental energy, skipping down the river banks smiling with the water and flowers and dragonflies. Nothing mattered because everything was in a perfect flow. He soared high up into the bright blue sky and came back around, approaching the right branch of the river. Instantly, things began to feel forced and unnatural. There was no dragonflies and the river labored over rocks and fallen logs. Knowing exactly what to do, he returned to his body sitting beside the fork in the river.

Smiling, he stood from his meditation and set off down the bank of the left river. As he walked, the landscape ahead started changing. The icy mountain terrain slowly gave way to more exposed rocky outcrops and the rocky outcrops slowly turned to rock and sand. Before long, he was entirely surrounded by desert.

Looking back, he could no longer see anything but desert. The mountain he had been on was completely gone from his view and rather than some alternate version of the Cascade Range of Northern California, it was as if he had been trekking across the Mojave Desert of Southern California the entire time. In a way, he found this strangely comforting.

The only aspect of the landscape that struck him as extremely odd was the river. The cobalt blue water remained unchanging as it snaked along through the great desert. Aside from any misgivings he had about being lost in the desert of a strange world, he took comfort in his vision from earlier; in knowing that all he had to do was follow the river and it would guide him to exactly where he needed to be.

After several hours of walking the desert scape, he decided to rest and take stock. He was uncertain of where he was headed, but he had come to trust his decision to continue along the river. He had no concept of how far he had traveled. Now, he was back in the moment, and the moment stretched outward into the vast infinite.

Off in the distance, far from the river bank upon which he currently stood, he saw the outline of what appeared to be a person. Without really understanding how, he had a knowing in his heart that it was time to leave the river behind for a little while. He stepped off in this new direction, heading away from the river and surprised himself when he started humming.

Being so much more in touch with the emotions he was feeling at any given point, he recognized that he was excited about interacting with another person for the first time in weeks. Although he had been in continual conversation with the energy of the Elders during his time at the cave, it just wasn't the same as sitting in front of another person and communicating freely.

Strangely, he noticed as he progressed toward the figure standing out in the desert that he wasn't so much moving over the landscape as the landscape was coming toward him.

He remembered a time when he was a very active runner, and would race ultra-marathon distances on wilderness trails. Several times he had experienced a very mild version of this sensation, yet he had always dismissed it as nothing more than a trick of the fatigue he was feeling at the time. He had tried unsuccessfully on several occasions to meditate on the concept that no one ever moves about physically in the world. That we are all the exact centre of our own personal version of reality, and that the reality actually moves and bends around us instead.

Now that he was so much more connected to the feeling, he said to no one in particular "maybe there was something to it after all."

After what appeared to be an age of walking through the sandy desert, he finally started to see the details of the person he was heading toward, and realized with a little buzz in his stomach that it was Mara. She stood up next to a pile of sticks and logs that she had amassed next to a little circle made from rocks.

"Your timing is perfect," she shouted across the remaining space to him with a laugh. "I've just finished preparing for your arrival."

As he finally closed the space between them, he looked a little baffled. "Um, Mara? It's wonderful to see you of course, but I had to make several decisions at various crossroads along my journey in order to get here. How did you know that I would choose to take the paths I did and arrive at this exact spot?"

She smiled in that funny little way of hers that melted his heart each and every time he gazed upon it. "My beautiful friend, there is much we need to talk about. Help me get this fire started so that we can sit and speak freely of such things and more."

He picked up the kindling and smaller sticks and made a little pyramid out of them in the middle of the stone circle while she lit them, apparently with nothing more than her thoughts. Once the fire started, they sat together in silence, staring at the bright orange and yellow element flickering in front of them. He noticed that the light around them was growing less bright, although it wasn't the same as the cycles of day and night like he had experienced at the cave with the Elders. There was no end to the moment they were currently in; it was more like the way the light faded in the grassy rest areas back at the forest so that one could more easily go within and reflect.

"Nothing happens by chance alone," Mara almost sung the words to him. "Every Cause has its Effect and every Effect has its Cause; everything that happens, does so according to Law; When we speak of Chance, it is nothing more than a name for Law not yet recognized; of course, there are many planes of causation, but nothing escapes the Law."

He sat with a puzzled look on his face. "Mara, what does that actually mean?"

"It means that the choices you made in coming here were all part of something greater. To the casual observer, it may seem the paths you took were all random, yet if you look at how it actually happened, you will see that each time you had to decide on which course to take, you made the decision from a place of stillness... from within your own heart. In doing so, you moved above personality and ego, connected with the Flow of Universal energy and your decision became a part of Universal Law."

"In other words, you're saying that because I followed the paths that seemed a little brighter to me, that I was following the 'right' course?"

"Try not to think in terms of 'right' and 'wrong.' Rather, know that nothing happens by chance. This is such a beautiful understanding to come to because it allows us to see that there are definite patterns which govern the way things turn out. We are never just blindly left to find our way through a world of chaos. Once we come to fully understand the Principle of Cause and Effect, we can see how one thing gives birth to another, and find the connection in everything."

"I'm not sure I entirely understand," was all he could say.

She continued with a firmness in her voice he hadn't heard before. "When we connect to the Universal Law, we have the ability to see how one thing will trigger another, how one process or event preempts and leads to something else. This not only gives us a real empowerment in determining how things will turn out ahead of time, it also gives us the ability to change the past, much like you learned with the Elders back up at the cave. It is also how I knew you would find your way to this exact point."

He took a moment to ponder this. "The energy of the Elders mentioned that this process of changing the past would be covered in greater detail when I learned about the Principle of Cause and Effect. Although I have an understanding of it now, are you able to give me your wisdom about how it works?"

"Of course. When we change how we perceive the events that have already come to pass, we actually change what has happened. Perception alone is the filter that determines the reality we experience. You know that when you focus on something, you see plenty of that thing everywhere you go. Once we have the gained the ability to shift the way we see something that we always viewed as a setback as something helpful instead, then we have changed what happened from 'negative' to positive."

"I honestly feel that this is one of the most powerful tools I have ever been given," he said. "It no longer matters what happens, or even what has happened in life, because all of it is now within my ability to change, just by changing how I look at it."

"YES!" beamed Mara. "Life is much like a Lenticular printing. You can alter the image you perceive by shifting your perspective of it."

"Mara, tell me more about Cause and Effect. I don't feel like I have an adequate understanding of it yet."

"You actually know it as intimately as I do, you just don't yet trust your own understanding of it," she replied to him. "YOU tell ME more about Cause and Effect. The best way to learn anything is to teach it."

He thought on this for a few moments before slowly beginning, weighing each word with careful regard.

"Well, I guess in order to completely understand the Principle of Cause and Effect, we need to look at how one thing leads to another; that the end result of *anything* is nothing more than the product of what initially went into it combined with any changes that have been made along the way." As he spoke, he felt the words flowing through him in the same relaxed fashion that a deep river slowly meanders through a canyon.

"That's a *very* good start," Mara replied. "But go on... go deeper"

Trusting himself more and more with every word, he continued. "Anyone who says that the result of anything is unknown or random is actually only stating that they don't fully understand what the starting parameters were, or are unaware of the choices leading to any changes that were made along the journey toward the outcome. When one has a complete understanding of the start of anything, and also knows exactly what decisions were made and why, then a complete understanding of any outcome is forged." He drew a sharp inhale as if he had just spoken a truth that was far beyond his comprehension.

"You got it in one try, my dear friend," Mara said. "The best bit of the entire Principle is that it is a process not requiring one to be already at the outcome. That is why I was able to know without any doubt that you would take the paths you took, make the choices you made, and arrive at this place just the way you did."

CHAPTER 11

The Final Principle

"Every moment was a precious thing,
having in it the essence of finality."
Daphne du Maurier

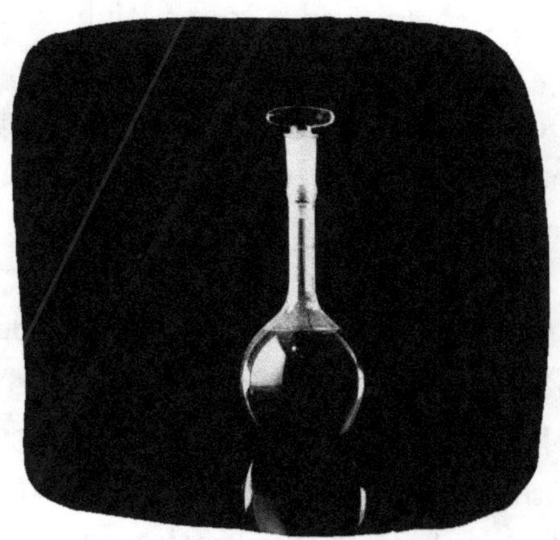

They sat in silence for some time. Both were able to enjoy each other's thoughts without speaking, yet neither of them thinking about anything more serious than the fire, the rocks, the warm desert air and the pleasant company.

Finally, he broke the silence. "Mara, as glad as I am for it, can I ask you why it was you that met me out here and not Sol?"

Her face light up as she replied, "Absolutely. For two reasons actually. One, Sol is busy preparing for the next part of your journey, and two, the final Universal Principle calls for an intimate understanding of the connection between all things. There is an inherent attraction that exists in the Universe, an attraction that draws everything toward everything else. The thing about this attraction is that it originates from the Divine Two."

"What do you mean the Divine Two?"

"The entire Universe was forged from the One creating Two, and the Two creating everything else. The Divine Two refers to the Sacred Feminine and Masculine Principles. For me to deliver this wisdom to you rather than Sol, we are in a far better position to explore the truth of the Divine Two."

He swallowed the lump that had been steadily growing in the back of his throat as she spoke, not entirely certain if his discomfort was as palpable to her as he perceived it to be. Right at that moment she laughed, and then with a look of deep concern, she tapped him on the knee and said, "Don't worry so much, my beautiful friend. Everything is exactly as it is meant to be."

He relaxed a little and she went on. "Tell me what you know about gender."

He pondered for a few moments. "As far as I understand it, gender refers to the differences between men and women, right? Not merely in terms of biological differences, but in social aspects or standing as well."

She gave him the kind of amused yet compassionate look that a parent gives a child who has presented their very best answer to a difficult question yet fallen a long way short of making any real sense.

"You have barely scratched the surface. Of course, on a purely superficial level you are correct. Gender does indeed refer to the differences between men and women, both biologically and socially. Yet, to make such a statement without going any deeper is akin to stating that a jungle is just a bunch of trees. What you are essentially doing is stating that the massive web of life that inhabits the jungle is nonexistent. It is only when we dig deeper that we start to see that there is so much more to it."

He felt the kind of disappointment that one generally gets when they don't have all the answers to something they're somehow supposed to have. "I guess they forgot to teach us that in college when they covered basic biology."

At that, her face lit up. "Right! Biology. Yes! Think back to the classes you had about cell structure. What do you remember?"

He thought about his days as a college student. He had attended a private institute to study Western Herbal Medicine. However, the first two years of his degree had included classes covering the same subjects as the first two years of any of the body-science degrees: Chemistry, Biology, Anatomy, and Physiology.

"Well, I guess at the most fundamental level, cells contain genetic information that determine a host of factors, including whether they are 'male' or 'female.' The Chromosome of the cell is what gives it a gender, so to speak."

He looked at her expectantly, pleased with himself at the knowledge he was still able to regurgitate regarding a difficult scientific topic he covered over 10 years ago.

"Again, you are technically correct. However, there is still so much more. Now, what I want you to do is to keep the same understanding firmly anchored in your mind and stop thinking about it the way that a scientist would. Find that space where the critical mind of a scientist gives way to the wondrous mind of a child. It is in that space alone that all answers can truly be understood perfectly."

They sat in silence for a long while as he thought about this. She knew the process that was unfolding within him and merely observed his mind with the curiosity of one who sat observing a butterfly emerge from a cocoon—all while knowing exactly how the story ends.

He glanced at her and noticed that she was staring intently at him with the corner of her lips turned up in a slight smile. "Go on. Tell me," She said.

He stared off for a moment, and then suddenly looked right at her with a clarity in his eyes that she had been waiting for this entire time.

"The Divine Feminine and Masculine are contained within everything, from the protons and electrons in a cell to a man and woman procreating in order to create new life.

The entire Universe was created on the energy of One creating Two and Two creating everything. This understanding permeates across every religion and doctrine of thought from the ages of humankind. We can also see how this reinforces the first great Universal Principle and the fact that the Universe has been created as nothing more than a projection of the mind of The ALL. There is only God. For there to be anything else, including a female with which God procreated in order to create life, would make that anything else 'not God.' The fact that in our physical Universe two come together to pro-create new life shows us that although we are a part of The ALL, we are not the same as The ALL."

She was beaming at him by the time he had finished speaking. This was the point he had been driving toward his entire life. Just as two powerful energies that had spent an eon racing toward one another finally collide in a cataclysmic explosion, his full awareness exploded into the moment with nothing less than world shattering force. He intimately knew not only the Universal Principles, but the very face, mind, and heart of God in a single moment.

"I can see that there has been much written on the topic of gender, particularly focusing on the Sacred or Divine Feminine," he continued. "It appears to be a topic that has been heavily adopted by the new age movement, and unfortunately, in many cases people arrive at Goddess worship and feminine empowerment without understanding the depth behind it or the balance needed within it. Of course, after living through a heavily egocentric, male dominated world for the past several hundred years, it is little wonder that the softer, Feminine side is now being embraced by the human race."

His intensity lessened briefly. "I actually had this conversation with a female friend recently while we were watching a 'brown' movie..."

Without really knowing why, he had always referred to any movie that involved armor, swords, shields, and castles as "brown movies."

"She was saying that the very fact men fighting each other with sharpened pieces of steel until one of them was cut badly enough that they died was a serious piece of evidence that men should simply not be in charge." They both laughed at this.

Once the lightness of the moment passed, his previous intensity returned and he continued.

"The way that the human race has been in recent times is also a real example of the Principle of Rhythm at play in our lives. As a race, we focused for the longest time on male dominance, and now the pendulum has swung back towards embracing the feminine. What we need to understand however, is that as a race in order to move forward completely, we must find that place of balance where Divine Feminine and Masculine embrace one another to pro-create new life, support one another, balance one another and we then need to polarize ourselves in the space."

Her look towards him was now of a proud parent that had just seen their child win the spelling bee with a particularly troublesome word.

"Understandably, there is trepidation within many of us surrounding the embracing of a Divine Masculine because of the damage done via the egocentric male dominance across the ages. However, it is extremely important to remain mindful that when speaking in terms of the Divine or sacred aspects of Gender as this Principle does, neither Feminine nor Masculine is more important than the other, because without one, the other cannot exist."

He finished speaking and they sat looking at one another for the longest time; locked in a 'Soul Gaze', where two people stare into each other's eyes in complete silence for a period of time. In doing such a thing, he noticed that the cycle of his breathing was starting to match hers, and something intuitively told him that even his heartbeat was falling into rhythmic step with hers.

Finally, she broke the silence in his mind with the gentle touch of her thoughts. *'To truly come to a place of understanding this great*

Universal Principle, is to understand life itself! From the smallest building blocks of the most basic 'matter' to the most complex macrocosmic worlds, Gender is present as the basis for all creation. Being the final Principle, it encompasses elements of all the other Principles. You can only come to such a strong understanding of Gender, when you have gained a complete understanding of the first six Universal Principles.'

CHAPTER 12

The Akashic Records.

"If you can accept the indescribable nature of your true identity,
you unveil the mystery of life."
—— Akemi G

They ended up staying together at the little desert camp for what he guessed was about a week. As there were no actual cycles of time, it was impossible for him to tell with any accuracy, however Mara made a point of having him light the fire periodically and during these times, the light radiating from within everything around them went dull just as it did when he first arrived. In doing so, they actually made their own cycles of day and night which he found was quite pleasant.

During their 'daylight' hours, they would walk amongst the dunes, meditate, practice a Yoga flow and generally spend time being active. Once they sat down beside the fire and the light would go dull, they would talk and Mara would challenge him and his understanding of the Universal Principles. The one thing that stood out to him as extremely unusual throughout the entire time was that the little stack of firewood never seemed to diminish. Neither he nor Mara replenished it, and despite burning it all the time, it was always there. He made a mental note to ask her about it when they spoke next.

One particular "morning" he awoke after a brief nap to discover that Mara wasn't there with him. He jumped up and having looked around in all directions, couldn't see her anywhere. Without really knowing what to do next, he sat back down next to their little fire pit, and noticed that there was an arrow drawn in the sand. After the quiet time that he had shared with Mara and following on from the predictable pattern they had embraced as a 'daily' routine, he felt a little touch of excitement by the prospect that he was about to have another adventure.

Stepping off in the direction that the arrow indicated, he walked for some time across the desert sands. As he progressed deeper into the desert and further from the river, he started musing that under any other circumstance, he would have been terrified to lose sight of the only landmark in such a vast desert. However today he trusted completely in Mara's guidance.

After a while of walking over nothing but sand and rock, cresting hills and dropping into valleys, he came upon one particular hill and saw a grove of palm trees appear in the distance. His intrigue spiked and he instantly became gripped with such excitement at what lay ahead, that he hurried his pace until he was almost running.

Having no real way of judging distance out in the desert of this strange world, he found himself much further out from the grove than he had anticipated when he had first laid eyes on it. As such, he found himself gradually slowing his pace right back down due to the fact that his brisk walking in the soft sand made for hard going, and his deep breathing told him without doubt that he was no longer a spectacle of fitness.

As he drew closer, he was able to start making out individual trees as well as a couple of small, hut like structures. Other than the trees themselves, there was no sign of life at this stage, yet he felt in his heart that he was to meet someone here and more to the point, that it would be a very important encounter.

After what he guessed at being several hours since he set out from his little desert camp, he finally made his way into the canopy of the palm grove. He delighted in being around the trees after such a long time away from them. 'How long had it been since he set forth at Sol's bidding from the top of the falls?' He felt from within himself that he had been gone for months now. So much had come to pass, and such a journey he had taken.

'Such a journey indeed my friend, and far you have come. Yet all of that was just the beginning, laying the foundation of understanding for what comes next. Now is when the real work begins.'

"SOL!" He exclaimed out loud excitedly. His tall guide stood in front of him and yet, he had no questions about how Sol had materialized out of thin air to be here in this place with him.

"It is SO good to see you."

Sol laughed out loud before returning to using his customary mind talk. *'You have done a marvelous job my friend. There have been many trials that you overcame to be here with me.'*

After his initial burst of excitement wore off, he went back to using his thoughts to speak with as well, as was always customary in his interactions with Sol. *'So, what do you mean now the "real" work begins?'*

'Ahh, my friend. Your time here and everything that you have learned along your journey thus far has given you a new way of seeing things. That is fantastic and you have taken to it like a duck to water as the saying goes. However, as it always the case, changing the way we see something does nothing for us in and by itself. Within a month of returning to your world, you will be back in your rut despite the time you have spent here with us. Everything will have been for nothing, and without you having

the ability to impart we have taught you to others of Earth, your world will die not long after.

We cannot allow that to happen, because worlds such as yours that have the ability to sustain complex life are few and far between in the Universe. Remember, although the Universe is all in he mind if The One, we MUST act as if it is real. The only way for us to ensure that you return completely awake and do not slip back into your slumber is to complete your journey. You are now to undertake the Great Work of a Master Alchemist. Now, you commence the Magnum Opus.'

Sol led him through the trees to one of the huts that he had seen from out in the desert. Although on the outside it appeared to be nothing more than a modest little structure of wood and thatch, upon entering he was dumbfounded to find what he was faced with. It was one of the most lavishly decorated rooms he had ever seen. Deceptively larger on the inside, it was sprawling with rugs and tapestries, and had unusual laboratory equipment everywhere. There was a floor to ceiling bookcase along one entire wall which housed hundreds of ancient look-ing volumes written in many different languages.

The crowning piece that stood proudly in the middle of everything else was a crucible that had shiny gold pipes venting to the roof for preventing toxic gas build-up inside the chamber. Upon seeing this, he was struck by the absurdity of what he was actually looking at. The hut that he had entered out in the desert was made of wood, whereas this room that he currently found himself in was made from carefully laid grey stone. He could just as easily have entered into a castle in the middle of Europe, and this 'chamber' would have been right at home in such a setting.

The confusion at the stark difference gave him a slight vertigo. He became dizzy and scrambled to grab at a wall. In that moment he heard Sol's voice in his mind as if from down a tunnel.

Just breathe my friend. What you are experiencing is a blend between Cognitive Dissonance and Sensory Overload. Remember when you first came to this world, we had to walk for some time before arriving, even though we were already "here" so to speak?'

He nodded without saying a word as he focused deep into his breathing.

'What you are experiencing now is a VERY mild case of what would have happened if we had just appeared here from your world. Even after all of this time with us, your mind is still heavily programmed to require process in order to believe something is possible. You must take a journey before you can arrive somewhere.

You must study long and hard before you allow yourself to know that you can speak another language. To give yourself permission to do or know anything without the process is not just the reality of the Universe, but because of the Principle of Correspondence, "As Above, So Below. As Below, So Above", it is also the reality to ALL the various worlds of the Universe.

What you see around you is not contained within the hut that you entered into from the desert a moment ago. Yet if you step back through that door, at this stage you will find yourself back in the palm grove of the desert. This chamber is a very sacred space. It contains the entire records of the known Universe.'

'Sol, are you telling me...'

'Yes my friend. You are standing in the sacred chamber of the Akashic Records. This place is where all of the Master Alchemists across the various histories of the many worlds in the Universe have come to complete their Magnum Opus.'

Even if nothing else had managed to do so thus far, his mind was now sufficiently blown. Of course, he had heard of the Akashic Records before, but to be standing in an ACTUAL PLACE that contained the records; that was almost more than he was able to comprehend.

'We were uncertain how you would take arriving here. There was much debate amongst my people as to whether we should even try. You need to understand, all of the Master Alchemists that have previously come to this place had dedicated their entire life to the pursuit of Alchemy and by the time they were ready to take on the Magnum Opus, they already had the ability to "make changes" without the need for process. This is also the reason that we needed you to find your own way here, overcoming the obstacles that were presented, and following your heart so perfectly as you

did. Ultimately, if you had turned any other way than you did at any point along your path, it would have taken you right back to the falls and the journey would have ended.'

After everything he had just heard, he only had one question for his guide. *'Sol, is the entry to the Akashic Records the same for everyone? Is it always through a hut in the desert?'*

'Usually, but not always. The way in requires a very similar journey and set of trials to what you faced. However, it is the way out that is far more interesting.'

His face creased into a puzzled expression. *'What do you mean, "The way out?" What happens on the way-out Sol? Do I not just pass back into the desert?'*

'Once your work here is complete, you have become a Master Alchemist. The irrefutable Universal Principles and Laws are still in effect of course, however you will have complete understanding of how to use one to overcome another, so to speak. "Reality" as you know it becomes a mere suggestion, and your will becomes LAW. When you come to leave here, that doorway which you came through will take you anywhere you wish to go.'

Without having Sol explain things any further, he knew exactly what was meant and was extremely grateful that everything worked out the way it did. He somehow knew within his heart that this was always the way of it though; when one is able to flow with the rhythm of immense gratitude, it's usually always because one has aligned with one's Heart Path.

CHAPTER 13

Magnum Opus

To know how to grow old is the master work of wisdom, and one of the most difficult chapters in the great art of living.
Herman Melville

Sol led him to a corner of the chamber where there were thick rugs adorning the floor and comfortable cushions lying about. He was prompted to take a seat, and lowering himself into a cross legged position opposite Sol, they began.

'In your world, the art and science of Transformational Alchemy has always remained hidden to all but the innermost sanctum of its learnings, and it was always thought to be referred to in an extremely complex

code in order to prevent common people from understanding and abusing the power behind it. The reality of the situation however, as with everything, is far simpler. Those that truly understood the process of Alchemy described it in a language that made sense to them at the time.

It saw a rise in use and understanding during an era when wisdom was actively hunted down, seized and repressed by power hungry clerics. It was a time where instead of embracing Universal wisdom, many people chose to remain ignorant rather than face persecution and almost certain death. To those that truly understood the Way, nothing was being hidden. They simply knew that unless someone was also initiated to their path, what was said and referred to really was nothing more than gibberish.'

'That explains so much about the history of Earth Sol. Concepts that have always appeared so complicated to understand, seem so simple when you explain them'.

Sol smiled briefly at this before continuing. *'Although there are numerous 'minor' processes of physical Alchemy, there is one major work, known as the Magnum Opus or Great Work. Although this was often thought to be the process for creating the philosopher's Stone, what completion of the Great Work gave the Master Alchemist was something far more powerful.'*

He looked at his guide with a puzzled expression. *'Tell me about the Philosopher's Stone Sol? I've heard of it but know next to nothing about it'.*

'Without going into too much detail, the Philosopher's Stone is a yellowish colored, malleable stone that just the smallest sliver shaved from has the ability to transmute anything from its base starting point, into perfection. It was often worked for and sought out as it was believed that it had the power to turn common lead into valuable gold.

The gross misconception right from almost the beginning of the Alchemist journey was that this process was something more than it truly is; and yet, to the any Alchemist who has successfully managed to navigate the 'gibberish' and found understanding within it, there was a prize far greater than all of the gold on the planet.

My friend, by the time we have completed this process here, the entire journey of your life will have changed course now from passenger to pilot, from victim to master, from casual observer to Divine Co-Creator.'

CHAPTER 14

Solutia

"Dissolution or liquidation of the Materia Prima"
"Everything is liquid and in constant motion but what we hold as solid within ourselves. Such things need to be returned to liquid for the world to start making sense once again; for the Principle of Vibration to govern as it should."

Sol stood from his seated position and walked over to the crucible in the middle of the room. With a wave of his hand, a fire instantly roared to life inside of it. He then moved easily over to a small table against one wall that held a stack of smooth, grey bars which appeared to be metal bricks. Taking one, he made his way back to the crucible and beckoned his Apprentice to join him as he started to speak.

'You are all born into the world as something whole; this is the reality of your world as it currently stands. You are born completely without fear, in trust and love of who you are. You trust this because you simply don't know any differently. As you don't yet know who and what you are and have no comprehension of what it means to be "alive", you accept yourself completely for anything that you might currently be, and in a subconscious state you are at peace with the Universe for there is not yet any measure of contrast or comparison.'

As Sol spoke the words without actually speaking, directly inserting the thoughts into the mind of his Apprentice, he placed the dull metal brick into a containment vessel within the crucible. As he did so, his entire arm was placed into the roaring fire up to his elbow. He carefully sat the brick down onto the base plate and slowly took his arm back. As if nothing had happened, he went to continue speaking but was interrupted by the alarmed sound of his Apprentice's voice. "Sol? How is your arm not burned to a crisp?"

Sol calmly replied with his melodic voice, "Think back to your lessons on the Universal Principles, specifically Vibration. Nothing rests, everything vibrates. So imagine for a second that my arm is nothing more than a particular vibration of energy, and the fire is also a vibration of energy that would otherwise have the ability to change the vibration of my arm via their interaction. This can only happen *if I allow it to!* By using one Principle against another; Law against Law, I am able to maintain the vibrational rate of my arm where I want it, without it being changed by an external force."

As they spoke, the metal brick started to become soft and made its way along the vibrationary rate towards liquid as it slowly melted inside the containment vessel of the crucible.

'The beginning of our journey my friend, takes us back to a space where everything is possible; where the world is full of wonder, ready to be explored and every breath is felt in the moment at which it is breathed. The beginning is, as you might guess, your childhood! You see, to the mind

of a child everything sits in a place of total amazement. It is such a state of amazement in which the journey of your life began, and believe it or not also the state to which an Alchemist must return in order to begin the Master Work.

Close your eyes and breathe. Go within. Hold within yourself an understanding on the deepest level that everything is possible based on your current position, and that with the correct process, the conditions for which your outcome will be cultivated are also already present. Unlike the child which doesn't even consider such things when creating their fantasy worlds, which are most definitely very real to them, the Alchemist has considered potentiality and has then chosen to move above it; such is the power in the mind of a Master Alchemist.'

For a brief moment he was jolted back to that unusual conversation in which he had spoken about potentiality in his session with his counselor. Had he known somewhere within himself back then, which seemed like many months ago but was in fact only earlier the very same week, these concepts that Sol was now referring to? As he and his guide were so deeply connected in their minds, Sol paused to allow the thought to play out for him before continuing.

'This is a state that is not exclusive to young children and Master Alchemists; we all have the potential to exist in such a state, and it is this very space to which all will return in time.

To the mind of an Alchemist attempting the Master Work, just as to the mind of a child entering the world, everything is one and the same and therefore it does not matter where we begin the process or what we begin it with; it can be a bar of lead, or it can be the petals of a flower. It has always been traditionally believed that the Master Work was a process that could turn lead into gold. Transmuting a base metal into the precious is very much a reality, of course, as long as we are able to shift our perspective enough to completely understand on an inherent level that lead already contains the same building blocks as gold, and that a common street criminal already contains the same building blocks as a monk.

I want you to remain mindful of one thing whilst doing this work. When you come to the point that you are able to shift your perspective so as to see that lead and gold are one and the same, then the Master Work is already complete within you and you have made the ultimate transmutation... yourself.'

The lead had all but completely melted into a state of liquid on the base plate of the crucible by this stage, and once again Sol started to speak within the mind of his apprentice.

'The lead has been reduced to a state of liquidity now because the vibration of the fire is stronger than the vibration that holds the bar as a solid. This is the way of things. The stronger vibration exerts its will upon the weaker.

Remember back to the times of extreme trauma in your life my friend. The situation outside of you was vibrating higher than the rate at which you could hold yourself, so just as the fire melted this bar of lead, the circumstances in your life at the time melted you. The elements of the base materia that do exhibit a high vibration remain, whilst everything else is burned away. Know that this is a perfect thing and that it must happen this way.'

'Why Sol? Why do we have to endure so much hardship in order to grow?'

'It is the nature of the Universe, nothing more, nothing less. Look at those bars of lead stacked over on the table in the corner. We can do nothing with them until they are first melted. You are the same my friend. Until a situation outside of yourself has forced you to examine all of your current paradigms, you don't even know that work needs to be done.'

Sol paused long enough for this understanding to sink in, and then continued.

'This liquidation must occur, for it is impossible to work with something at its most fundamental level whilst it remains in a complete and complex form. A metal cannot have one or more of its elements isolated and removed whilst it is still solid.'

Accessing his most painful memories, Sol hammered the point home, *'For you, it happened that the time you started having panic attacks around your 16th birthday was because the paradigms that you had always used to define your world had been slowly melting away without you even noticing it. Because of the series of emotional traumas that you had been through, your life had been placed in the crucible that night, and you were slowly heating up and melting because of it. Of course, you couldn't have known then and there that you had been living your life for years in a state of slow yet definite dissolution.'*

He remembered the night that he had awoken to his first panic attack. Everything around him, including the very air itself, was pressed up close, throbbing, pulsating, invading his space and threatening his sense of identity. He had no point of reference, as the "self" that he had known before he'd drifted off to sleep had completely dissolved.

Everything was so much larger, brighter and more "in his face" than he remembered falling asleep to, and he had a kind of super awareness of everything. The LED clock told me him that it was 1:09am, and Billy Idol was happily belting out about White Weddings via the radio which had been left quietly playing in the background.

As he glanced over the vivid memory, he found himself pondering whether the bar of lead felt the same way when it was placed into the crucible to be melted.

Sol dragged him from his memory with words cutting into his thoughts like a skilled butcher slicing meat from the bone. *'Although this first stage of the Master Work is one of the most dramatic, it is completely necessary in order to create a state with which the materia can be worked with. The reason that the first step of the Master Work of Alchemy in dissolving the base materia from a solid into liquid is so that the complexities of the whole become simplistic, basic and fundamental.*

Now, find yourself somewhere comfortable and take rest. You are going to be here for a long and difficult journey'. Without another word, Sol disappeared from the chamber leaving the fire burning brightly within the furnace.

CHAPTER 15

Putrefactio

The Raven - Burial of the dead into the Earth
"Blackening (A descent into the nether sphere) in which the
materia becomes black or putrid"
The event that separates the components of the liquid self, takes the
pieces and burns away the impurities; the process of which blackens all of
the pieces of the whole, and allows only those of value to be restored to
purity.

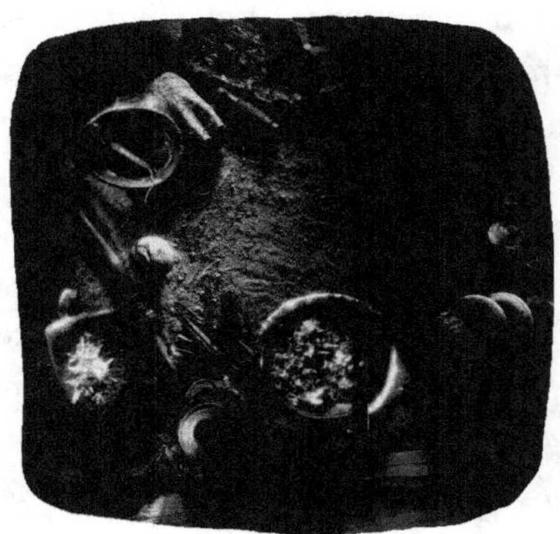

Over the next several days, he was left to his own devices. He used the time to rest, meditate as he had been shown by Mara during their time at the desert camp, and read through some of the volumes of books that adorned the almighty bookcase. He was fascinated to find that there was a book covering any subject he could imagine, and that all he needed to do was hold a topic in his mind of what he wanted to learn more about, and a book spine would start to glow somewhere in the giant library.

Although there were still no cycles of time, it felt to him that maybe a week had passed since Sol had left. He made his way over to the furnace in the middle of the chamber and looked into the crucible. He noticed with surprise that the entire mass of liquid metal in the bottom of the containment vessel was no longer grey yet rather was blackened and approximately only a third of the volume was remaining from what had been there when they had first started.

He was brought from his focus on the metal back to the chamber by Sol's voice in his mind.

'Once the Alchemist has dissolved the base metals in the crucible, they will continue to keep the fire burning bright, hot and strong on the now liquid metal so that all of the impurities will slowly burn away. There is an understanding by those on the path of the Alchemist that the process by which fire purifies is in its interaction on a vibrationary level with the materia it is burning. If something holds a lower vibration than that of the fire, then it will be consumed, and whilst anything with a higher vibration than the fire will also be blackened, it will ultimately remain.'

He nodded that he understood and Sol continued, *'In Alchemy, Putrefactio is the stage of the Master Work where all of the impurities are revealed so as to be burned off. This is where the materia is subjected to phenomenal heat, being that although EVERYTHING becomes blackened, the impurities alone will be destroyed by the fire whereas everything of value remains fundamentally unchanged. Traditionally, this meant creating an environment in which the base materia was melted down during the stage of Solutia, and that which was of no value to the end process of the work was burned away by the process.'*

Sol looked deep into him with a blazing intensity in his eyes. *'I want you to remember that the night you awoke to your first panic attack was merely when you became aware that you were melting in a crucible. The reality is, you had been placed into the fire many years prior to that, and it took that long for you to catch on.'*

He instantly knew that Sol was referring to the day that he brought his Mother's affair to light. That was the moment he was placed into the fire.

Sol left from the chamber again without saying anything else. It was like this now; coming and going without word, no friendly conversation, no space to discuss anything other than what was happening in the fire, and the comparisons that Sol was drawing between that and his life.

He went to the giant library wall and held in his mind a loose thought on real alchemy. Within a few moments, a book spine started to glow, so he reached up and pulled it free from its home. Turning the ancient volume in his hands he read the title aloud "Beyond the Fire - The Alchemist's Path of Profound Transformation."

His own voice sounded strange in his ears as he had only used it a couple of times since arriving all those months ago.

Opening the book randomly, he smiled at how things worked in this unusual place as he read:

There is a particular event that happens in our lives, just one event that stands out above all others. It is a truly wonderful thing, but more often than not it is disguised as a deeply traumatic situation that shapes what is to happen on the path of our lives for a long while to come. Although we are not able to see it as such in the moment, and sometimes not ever in a single lifetime, even the most horrific of events is a beautiful gift.

For the first time in his life, he was able to look at the day that he told his Father about his Mother's affair and see it as a beautiful gift, rather than a horrific mistake. He threw his head back and roared into laughter. Each time he started to settle, he laughed even harder until his mid-section was cramping in pain at the exertion of laughing so much for so long.

Eventually he was able to continue reading:

This event is obviously quite different for everyone but if you take a moment to glance back along your life path thus far, you will know the one to which I refer. There are instances however, where such a thing can be so traumatic that we may have blocked it out from our conscious mind so completely and therefore without out-side assistance it may very well sit beyond the scope of our conscious memory.

Having said that, I can promise you one thing: This event has been defining and influencing the choices that you have made, the relationships that you have forged, even the jobs that you have ended up in across your entire life. Because of having lived through and survived the gift of the Putrefactio event, you see the world completely differently and you are in fact blackened in one way or another because of it.

He sat down onto a plush rug in the corner of the library area and kept reading:

After the process of Dissolution, the intense heat of the crucible like environment of our lives is maintained. It is here that the parts of our melted self from the dissolution stage are all subjected to this incredible heat in a fire designed to destroy everything that doesn't serve us. As such, we are left in a state of almost total bewilderment. The core of our very nature is blackened by the stress we have just endured, and whether we are able to recognize it in the moment or not, everything that can not serve us in moving forward is burned away by the process.

Unfortunately, many of us tend to cling to the pain of the fire, we tend to cling to our old identities, we cling to those parts that don't serve us which are being removed from us and very quickly we step from the crucible with nothing more than charred remnants of our old life. Of course, the valuable elements are still there awaiting us to finish the work, but the process was too painful and hasn't been completed.

The worst thing that anyone can do to themselves is to give up on the journey at this stage. It happens more often than not though because of our inability to see what has happened as a gift rather than the curse that we tend to view it as.

He drifted off into a deep slumber whilst lying propped up reading and started dreaming almost immediately. He dreamt that he was curled up on the couch as a young child watching the news on the TV with his Mother. Something horrible had happened, and the news was making short work of reporting it. He caught the details, something about a man that had tortured and killed a small child that he had abducted from a local shopping mall.

He saw his Mother shake her head, asking in disbelief *'What kind of monster could do such a thing?'* The next scene on the TV was in front of a courthouse, with a mob of angry people screaming that this man should be put to death for his crimes. Although he apparently didn't understand it at the same level that the grown-ups seemed to, as saddened as he was for the child that died, he found himself feeling even more so or the man that had committed the crime. That poor tortured soul.

The next moment, the lounge room and his mother and the TV all slipped away into darkness. His dream took on a strange quality, almost as if he could taste the air itself. He found himself standing in the cave of the Elders up at the fork in the river, however this time he wasn't alone yet surrounded by tall, serene looking beings emanating a soft light.

As if they had been in the lounge room with his Mother and him watching the TV, they started to speak aloud about the man that had been at the centre of the events he had witnessed on the screen.

"He entered into his personal Putrefactio and instead of allowing himself to move through it and onto the next stage of the work, the stage that polishes and creates purity within once again, he stayed blackened; he moved away because of his fear and allowed the blackened and charred parts of himself that would otherwise have been removed throughout these steps to become his identity. Understand this, and forever you will maintain compassion for all, no matter what action they place upon the world."

He was heartbroken that instead of the man's actions being met with a compassionate desire to understand and help relieve the suffering he was experiencing, everywhere people start screaming for him to be punished. Again the Elders in the cave spoke, *"It is NOT the truth of our loving, caring nature that screams this but rather comes from our own unfinished work, from our own blackened state.*

We see reflected within this person's actions the darkness we carry within ourselves, the charred remains of our own impurities that we have buried deep within and we scream that punishment is the answer; if we were to acknowledge that they were truly in need of a compassionate and understanding hand, then we are also admitting that there is work to be done within ourselves."

The cave scene and the Elders faded in front of him, and for a moment he was suspended in the darkness of the void. In a single moment there was an explosion of Light all around him and he felt himself expanding beyond the physical limitations of his body, blending with the energy of Light. He awoke still propped up in the corner of Akashic chamber. As he opened his eyes he realized that Sol was sitting with him and had his hands cupped around his head.

It had felt like a month had passed since Sol had shown him anything other than a strict, business-like approach to the Magnum Opus process they were working through. This visit however, it was different. His guide was pouring love and compassion into him after his experience with the Elders, which had left him shaken.

It was one of the rare instances that Sol actually used his voice, however in doing so it had a profoundly calming effect on him.

"I'm going to explain exactly how someone steps from the fire of the crucible, an action which ends this Alchemical process prematurely. Because understanding this is the key to understanding many of the conditions that have plagued you and your world. As there is not actually a physical fire in which we remove ourselves from, yet rather a series of emotional, mental and psychological upsets, the way someone goes about stepping from the burn in order to reduce the pain is via distraction, addiction and accumulation. The work is ceased the second someone thrusts their focus in the direction of distracting themselves with TV, internet, Facebook, drugs, alcohol, endless shopping, accumulation of mountains of junk, gambling etc. Anything that prevents one from continuing to focus on the work at hand because it is becoming too painful."

As he sat there listening to his guide, he realized the truth of his life had not in fact been suffering at all as he had come to believe for so long now. He realized in that moment that he had been progressing down a path that led him to this very moment. At that, he fell back into a deep, dreamless sleep.

CHAPTER 16

Albedo

White Dove
"Lightening the putrid or blackened materia. It's made white and
pure again"
That moment, oh so sweet, when one realizes that one is in fact still
functioning and free to be happy within their own life. The emptiness!
The choice!

He came to slowly, at first not remembering where he was. When it finally dawned on him, he jumped up and raced over to the furnace. To his surprise, the fire had reduced right down to a mild flame, and what was remaining of the lead had re-solidified. Armed with a sense of deep understanding that had eluded him across his life, he reached into the crucible without fear of the flames and took the piece of lead in hand.

'Now you carefully "polish" the metal and the blackness of the impurities come away, but as the metal is still not quite solid, any contaminants introduced at this stage will require the entire process to start all over again.'

He heard Sol's words in his mind and knew that his guide had been standing right behind him from the moment he had come to the furnace.

'The next step of the Magnum Opus is known as Albedo, by which everything not destroyed in the fire of the crucible is restored to its individual purity. What we are therefore going to do is take what is remaining of this piece of lead that has been blackened by fire, and remove the residue of the impurities from it so that it returns to a shine of sorts.'

'Sol, how do I polish it?'

Sol took the piece of lead and placed it gently back into the containment vessel of the crucible. He produced a flask of liquid that had an opaque shimmer to it, and started to wash it over the small piece of metal. Instantly, the blackness gave way to reveal a low shine of silvery grey.

As he continued to douse the metal he spoke, *'You may notice that metals such as brass and copper, if left without constant care and attention will tarnish and turn green, even without interaction with fire. From an Alchemical point of view, this is due to the high content of impurities in the metal. Pure gold never tarnishes, not even over a thousand years at the bottom of the ocean, because it has no impurities in its composition that allows this to happen. Once any metal has been passed through the fire, and all of the impurities have been burned away, what remains will hold a very similar attribute in this respect to that of gold.'*

Sol left the chamber once again and left him to with the task of polishing the metal. Although the effects of removing the blackening and revealing the silvery grey of the metal itself were instantaneous, he had been instructed to keep going with it and maintain continued effort.

During a break from his task, he once again took *"Beyond the Fire - The Alchemist's Path of Profound Transformation"* down from the shelves of the library. Trusting that he would find what he needed, he randomly opened the book and read:

After the Alchemist has taken the base, melted it down into a state of liquidity and burned off the impurities, the remaining materia then needs to have its spirit restored. How this actually happened traditionally depended upon which Alchemist you spoke with. For the benefit of our personal path however, the restoration of spirit occurs in what we choose to do following interaction with the fire.

Having successfully come through the Blackening, one is left feeling completely discombobulated. There has been a process of having been pulled apart, burned, and certain parts of the self that have been used to negotiate the world for so long now have been destroyed in the fire. There remains a certain deep emptiness within.

One of two things will happen, either one will become so overwhelmed from the path thus far that once again it will be stepped from, allowing the new emptiness to fill with more dross from the world around so as to distract from the feeling of emptiness, OR a feeling of immense lightness at having released everything that no longer serves, thus commencing the process of polishing ourselves. If the latter is chosen, it is the polishing of the self that leads to the next part of the Master Work - Albedo.

After the base metal has been melted and the impurities burned away, the metal is allowed to cool a little. The heat in the crucible is still very intense by all standards and the metal is not permitted to solidify completely, however it is brought to a state similar to that of putty. It is in this state that the now purified metal can be effectively worked with through the remaining steps of the Magnum Opus.

He wasn't sure how it kept happening that every time he opened this book, it was right on the page that he needed to read. To test whether it was just this book in particular, or somehow something to do with what he was learning in the chamber, he grabbed another book randomly from shelf, opened it and read from a paragraph halfway down:

...this is usually the case when you observe people who appear to be stuck in the same behavioural patterns over and over again. We may ask, 'Why are you going back there when you know what awaits you?

Closing the book, he glanced at the title which read, *"Behavioral Patterns Exhibited During Intense Change."* He shook his head with a silly grin, knowing that what he had just read referred to what happens when someone allows impurities to enter back into their life after having gone through the fire.

Recollecting across the years of his life, he came to consciously know that it was never a smooth run through the processes for him. He remembered turning away from the path more times than he cared to think about; each time at best returning to the point at which he stepped away, but usually having to begin all over again. He also realized in that moment that of course, no one ever truly steps from the path, as this is simply not possible whilst staying alive on Earth. That we only tell ourselves we have done so by distracting ourselves from it. Yet each time we pause and choose distraction, we are held in a state of limbo until we make the choice to return to the work.

It was sometime later that Sol reappeared and asked him to go for a walk with him.

'You have been in the chamber working tirelessly for a long while now. It's time you came out into the world for a few moments.'

He noticed that his guide had a somewhat mischievous grin, however thought better of pushing the issue.

They stepped through the main doorway which had previously brought them directly into the records chamber from the desert. However, as they emerged, he found that they were now standing on the edge of a rocky outcrop, with a cliff immediately at their feet dropping away into the void. He imagined that if it hadn't been dark as the darkest night, they would have been surrounded by mountain ranges, yet he couldn't see anything beyond a few feet. As he glanced up, he breathed in the beauty of the starry sky, but noticed the further he tried to look outwards, the more the entire vista faded into a void of total nothingness.

Sol allowed him a few moments to take it all in before speaking.

'We are now standing on the edge of all reality. This is the great void from which creation comes forth. It is in this very spot that the first Beings of the Source dreamed the entire Universe into creation.'

He was rendered completely speechless. Never in his wildest imaginings had he thought that such a "place" could exist, let alone that he would find himself standing in the perfection of its presence.

'It brings a great deal into perspective, doesn't it my friend?' asked Sol with a smile. Again, all he could force himself to do was nod his agreement. He noticed with a little uncertainty that he was feeling somehow more "full." It was as if his arms, legs and torso were expanding outwards, and whereas once he had taken up only a very small part of the ledge they were standing on, he was now engulfing the entire area with his body.

Sol turned and walked back towards the doorway that they had emerged from, and disappeared from view. He knew in his heart that whatever was coming for him, whatever was about to happen, he had to face alone. A moment later there was an explosion of light that came forth from the void which knocked him backwards from his feet. He closed his eyes and braced himself to hit the hard stone of the ledge that he'd been standing on, however it was a sensation that never came. He instead found himself floating in complete darkness.

He gently opened his eyes and found that he was surrounded by the stars that he had been looking up at only a moment earlier. As he lay there floating in the nothingness, he started to hear what appeared to be musical sounds all around him. He soon came to realize that when he looked in the direction of a star, he would hear a particular note emanating forth from it. If he shifted his attention towards a different star, he heard another sound, and more so, if he pulled his gaze back to the entire vista, all of the notes of the individual stars blended into the most perfect symphony he had ever heard.

He laughed with joy, a deep soul laugh that sprung forth from every cell in him. He laughed not just at the immense beauty of the sound all around him but also at the understanding that each and every aspect of his being was nothing more than a product of the very same sound. In that moment, he knew he was home. Everything that had come to mean so much to him, all of the important aspects of his life such as the grievances of his job, the struggle to commute down the motorway, the frustration of struggling for parking of an evening, even his difficult past, all dissolved in the perfect sound.

What he came to understand in sharing space with the stars was that the intelligence of the entire Universe was also being carried on the sound he was hearing. As it flowed all around and through him, he knew for the first time in his life that the face he was gazing into, the very face of God, was also his own face.

It was either an eternity or a moment later that he felt something calling to him. He was being pulled in a particular direction and although every part of him wanted to resist and stay, he knew that there was a great need for him elsewhere. As soon as he had that one thought, he found himself standing back on the cliff edge with Sol beside him.

At this stage there was no need for words, either spoken or mentally transferred. Sol smiled, placed his hand over his apprentice's shoulder and led him slowly back through the doorway and into the chamber.

Once they were standing beside the furnace back in the chamber, Sol looked at him and said,

'There is something you need to know about human nature before this lesson is over. Unlike metal in which the impurities are completely gone during the burning process and only that which is pure is removed from the crucible, after the "burn" that people go through, humans tend to hold on to those parts of themselves that have been with them throughout their lives.

This is done even if those parts were impure or destructive; charred and burned, existing as nothing more than memories of the personality. Although the best option is not to engage with the mind over this and to just allow the process to unfold.

Somewhere deep within all humans, just as in the intelligence of the metal, you already know what will serve you as you step forward and what will not. Because this Alchemical process is almost a returning on an energetic level to your soul and cellular "blueprint," keeping the limited egoic self out of the process is the most empowering thing you can do.'

Citrinitatio

Peacock's Tail
"The materia must now be re-enriched by philosophical milk or
'Lacta Philosophica', the completion of which is the assumption of a
yellow color"
*Having sought outside of ourselves for everything that the truth isn't,
we are eventually driven within to a space of finding everything that the
truth is.*

Standing in front of the furnace with the now shining piece of lead
resting peacefully inside the containment vessel of the crucible, both
guide and apprentice had been silent for the longest time. He found

that since his experience on the ledge, that there was no need for Sol to talk him through any of the processes. It wasn't that he knew ahead of time, it was just that as he needed to know something, it was already there for him.

He knew in his heart that just because a particular base metal had been placed in a fire, melted, had its impurities burned away and then restored to solidity, didn't mean it was now gold. The building blocks were there of course, they always had been and without all of the impurities clouding it, the metal was so much closer in nature to that of gold.

However, he also understood that there was a process by which the metal needed to be "shown" the nature of gold within itself. Reaching deep into his own self, a process which had only just become available to him because of the connection he forged with himself whilst in the void, he discovered that there was a 'trick' used by Master Alchemists. The now pure metal is introduced to its own gold like nature via an interaction with an essence that currently differentiates it from gold - Lacta Philosophica.

He turned to Sol who without a word handed him a vial of milky gold liquid. For the first time since returning to the chamber, he spoke deliberate words out loud with absolute certainty and purpose.

"The interaction with this Philosophical Milk is not to chemically change the metal from the outside, but will show it that nothing was lacking from within itself in the first place. Nothing that is outside of itself can help it to become *more* than it currently is, except in demonstrating that it already is everything it needs to be! And so it is with the path of our lives too!"

As he applied the Lacta Philosophica to the lead, it immediately started to change. Although already a much shinier silver color than the drab grey of the original brick of lead that had been placed into the fire so long ago, it now slowly started becoming brilliant gold as the liquid washed all around it.

He reached into the furnace and took the small piece of gold metal into his hands. Although it had been sitting in a mild fire, it was cool to the touch, and he noticed that it was still a great deal softer than what a piece of metal should be. Turning to his guide, he nodded and without saying a word handed him the gold.

For the first time since they had met, he saw tears well up in Sol's eyes. *'My friend, you have truly come to a strong level of knowing. I am very proud of you.'*

CHAPTER 18

Destillatio

Red Dragon
"Reddening of the materia. Charging the re-enriched materia with sacred fire"
Everything that we have learned thus far, if allowed the space to do so, will charge us with a Divine fire of purpose so bright that nothing can diminish it.

He turned and faced Sol, nodded and simply said *'Let's complete the work.'*

His guide nodded in return and handed him the small piece of gold. He took the metal and continued speaking out loud words that he knew where his, yet did not come from within his mind.

"The final element of the work is to make still the new state of the metal. As yet the gold remains in a semi liquid state of putty, freshly cleansed of its impurities. In order to gain purpose, it now needs to become solid.

Regarding humans, at this stage we find ourselves growing into our spiritual maturity. During Albedo, we allowed ourselves to become empty. We started viewing the world with new eyes and as we moved into Citrinitatio, everything we interacted with captivated us as if we were children. Once we successfully managed to rise from the potential of falling into a world of "spiritual ego" and re-corrupting ourselves, we realized that it was *not* about what we could learn but rather what we could unlearn. Just as with the lead, it was never about what we could become, but rather unbecoming everything we are not."

Sol was absolutely beaming with delight. Not so much at the fact that his student had finally made the transition from apprentice to Master Alchemist in his own right, but that he was able to so skillfully draw the link between what was happening with the metal, and what occurs along the spiritual path of people. These understandings were an integral part in his return to his own world and being able to successfully guide others towards the light.

"By this stage anyone on the path has endured a great deal of hardship. Yet as long as we have been able to remain non-attached to the processes and just allowed them to occur with a relaxed observation, we were whisked along on the journey by the very processes themselves. We didn't have to actually DO anything in order to stand in the fire, to have our impurities burned away, to release the things that no longer served us. Once started upon, the process just 'happened' if we allowed it the space to do so, and we were taken along for the ride."

So what is the difference between that, and what comes next?' asked Sol, challenging his understanding.

"The difference Sol, is that this next stage of the path is where we find the real grass roots of integrating the spiritual journey into our everyday, mundane existence. It is a process that has the potential to drive one crazy time and time again. It can be a time of phenomenal despair, as the everyday human world will test and chip away at everything we have endured so much to build.

Someone that has journeyed so very far in order to arrive at this point has three options. They can either turn their back on the integration of their spiritual path and return to mundane life completely, they can embrace it entirely and decide to take on a monastic life, leaving the materialistic world behind, or they can practice diligently the things they have learned and allow themselves to *become* the path so as to guide others to the Light."

'The first two options are self-explanatory my friend, but tell me more about the third. How does one become their path?'

He grinned at Sol's challenge, knowing full well that his guide already knew the answer.

"Establishing a way of bringing oneself as an empty vessel into the world, not burdened with attachment or desire, can be extremely difficult. It isn't just about releasing that which we have loved and despised alike, but also letting go of the idea that we even walked a path at all to arrive at this point. Approaching the modern, material world as such an empty vessel is a challenge to say the least, yet if we allow this stage the space to 'work' within our lives, we will find that we start becoming an instrument of the Divine.

Essentially Sol, at this stage of the work we need to take our time to completely integrate our new spiritual way of being into the physical world, so that the concepts of both spiritual AND material dissolve and we just 'are.'"

With that, he turned towards Sol and held out his hand. In his upturned palm was a piece of brilliantly shining gold.

Tinctura

The Philosopher's Stone
"The completion of the Lapis"
The Stone only has a single purpose without which, it is nothing more
than a pretty rock!

Sol took the piece of gold from him and holding it up high above his head, softly spoke some words in a language that he had never heard. As he spoke, the gold start to glow. Taking his hands away and leaving the glowing piece of metal floating in mid air, he turned back to his now Master Student and said out loud, "There is a saying, 'You walk the Path until the point that you *become* the Path.'

The actuality of this is something that literally cannot be explained or understood beyond intellectual concepts until it is experienced. Having said that, the experience of such a thing is the accumulation of phenomenal work, spread potentially across countless lifetimes.

The point that I am making with this is simple: Once you have walked your path to the point that you are one with everything, once you have completed the Master Work, *you* yourself have become The Philosopher's Stone. My friend, you are now an agent for powerful and lasting change in everything that you come in contact with. Your only responsibility in remaining in the physical world is to facilitate this change wherever and whenever you can."

The piece of gold changed shaped so that it became a pendant of the Three Primes or Tria Prima, and floated gently back down into Sol's hand. He walked around behind his student and tied the pendant around his neck to be worn as a talisman.

'This serves two purposes. It is a key that will permit you entry to this chamber any time you desire. As you have come to learn, everything you need is on hand with but a thought. All you have to do is hold the thought of this place in your mind, and step through any doorway and the talisman will allow you to transcend Space/Time to arrive here. Secondly, it is to serve as your reminder of the work that you have done here. Know within yourself each time you gaze upon this talisman, that both it and you began here as lead.'

With that, Sol turned and walked from the chamber.

He sat for a few moments after his guide had left, recollecting everything that had brought him to this point. Although he knew his time in this mysterious land was coming to an end, for the first time in many years he felt a huge surge of excitement at what lay ahead.

CHAPTER 20

The falls

"Before Enlightenment, chop wood, carry water.
After Enlightenment, chop wood, carry water"
Zen Proverb

As he stepped through the doorway of the Akashic Records Chamber, he was a little surprised to find himself standing on a little quiet spot of grass not far from the top of the falls. Relieved not to have to make his way across the desert and up the river to the fork he sat on the grass and breathed out a big sigh of relief.

Somewhere behind him, he heard a familiar voice say "It works like that. Wherever your heart truly desires is where you end up upon stepping through the chamber doorway." He spun around and threw his arms around Mara with a huge smile on his face.

"It's *so* great to see you Mara!" he exclaimed with a genuine warmth radiating from his heart. She pushed him back for a second and looked at the talisman that hung down from around his neck.

"Well well" she spoke happily. "Master Alchemist then, is it?"

They both laughed playfully and out of nowhere, she tackled him into the pool. They swam and splashed and played without a care for what felt to be a pleasant eternity. Finally, she swam to the edge of the pool and said "I still owe you a walk down the fall path back to the bottom pool".

With that, he also made his way to the edge and they climbed out together. Hand in hand they made their way slowly down the winding trail. It was one of those moments that he experienced in his new home world, as he had come to think of it, that he wished would last forever. Together they had an amazing walk amongst some amazing old trees and made their way to the pool at the bottom of the falls.

After a long while of relaxing beside the water of the bottom pool and talking about his many experiences in the Akashic Chamber, she took his hand and led him through a part of the forest to a little clearing.

In the middle of the clearing was a long table, immaculately dressed and adorned with every type of food he had ever seen. The light emanating from everything in the clearing was dulled right down to create the sensation of evening, which even after all the time he had spent in this new world he still found strange because he had just stepped through the tree line from the brightness of daylight. All around the clearing were fire torches to create effect, and seated around the table were a dozen of the guides he had spoken to and worked with during his time here.

The head of the table was empty, as was one of the places to the side of it. At the other side of the head sat Sol, who smiled broadly when he saw his student appear. Mara lead him over by hand to the head of the table, and pulled his chair back for him to sit. As soon as he sat down, all of the guides stood in unison and began to clap and cheer.

Once the clapping had died down, all of the guides sat except for Sol. It was one of the rare occasions that he spoke out loud. "Tonight, we celebrate the newest entry into the Master Alchemists Guild. We have always stood to maintain the balance across the various worlds of this Universe, and in its greatest time of need, Earth has sent forth a candidate that has proven strong, capable and receptive."

He turned and faced the head of the table, "My student. Welcome home. Although you may return to this place whenever you choose, and I feel a very big part of your heart yearning to stay with us, you must now return and share what you have gained from your time here with the others of your world."

CHAPTER 21

The day after

"The secret of change is to focus all of your energy, not on fighting
the old, but on building the new."
Socrates

He slowly opened his eyes after what felt to be an amazing night of celebration with his new friends. At first, he couldn't make sense of his surroundings. He couldn't hear the sound of the falls in the distance, there was no soft grassy patch under him and he noticed that the light wasn't coming from within everything, yet rather from a single source overhead.

Blinking several times, he sat up and realized that he had been lying on a blanket of pine needles beside his tent. Looming above the trees in front of him was Mt. Shasta in all of its glory, and when he realized that it was only yesterday afternoon that he had sat down beside his tent and fallen asleep, he threw his head back and roared into a deep belly laughter.

He stood up slowly, breathing in the crisp mountain air and looked around at the vista as if he was seeing the world for the first time. Everything he gazed upon was somehow a little bit brighter than he had remembered from the day before, and if he didn't know better, he could have sworn that when he focused upon any one part of the landscape around him, he heard music softly emanating forth from it as if it sung in delight at being recognized by him. In that instant, he heard Sol's voice from within his head, *All everything wants is to be seen.*

He smiled continuously as he packed up his little camp with deliberate action. Every single movement had a purpose, and he felt each and every breath enter his lungs as he drew it in. Once it was all loaded into his pack, he shouldered the load and started the short walk back down to Bunny Flats. Within the hour, he was in his car on the motorway heading south.

Although the thought of heading back to LA should have depressed him, it simply didn't. He glanced down briefly and caught a glimpse of shiny gold through the buttons in his shirt and realized that regardless of what came next, he was ready.

CHAPTER 22

Afterword

The way forward

We are all Alchemists. From the very first step that we take on the path of the Alchemist, which is nothing more than the Spiritual Path and commencing on the day of our birth, we are moving in a continual direction towards self-perfection. We break down, separate, refine, purify and then put ourselves back together with a constant vigilance that we may not have ever consciously known.

Everything that we do, and everything that "happens" to us, is a vital part of the process towards elimination of the dross, and eventual perfection of the self. Many people look towards the difficult elements of the journey and feel that life has been unfair, or that these experiences were a waste of our time and life because we didn't enjoy them.

We tend to make a solid effort in hiding ourselves from our pain with things such as distraction, addiction, or accumulation. We actively avoid the path and engross ourselves in television, video games, food, drugs and alcohol, exercise; anything that keeps us distracted from the reality of the path. Attachment to such a way of living is very much a trap!

An even greater trap though, is to feel the beautiful and pleasant elements of our journey; those moments of bliss and spiritual connection and cling to them, crave them, and refuse to be at peace when they leave us. There is real danger in seeking for these feelings and experiences, because although they feel wonderful, they are still an element of the illusionary world and by chasing them we are in fact running back to the world of illusion.

The greatest action we can take upon the path to becoming the path, is to surrender. If it feels horrible, let it go. If it feels wonderful, let it go.

CHAPTER 23

Pub. Info